A GROUP

of

ONE'S OWN:

Nurturing the Woman Writer

❧ ❧ ❧

by

KAREN DESROSIERS

LAUREL LLOYD EARNSHAW

CHARLENE POLLANO

DEBORAH REGAN

SUSAN WERESKA

Story Line Press
2003

Published by Story Line Press,
Three Oaks Farm, PO Box 1240
Ashland, OR 97520-0055

www.storylinepress.com

This publication was made possible thanks in part to the generous support of the
Nicholas Roerich Museum, the Andrew W. Mellon Foundation
and our individual contributors.

Library of Congress Cataloging-in-Publication Data
A group of one's own : nurturing the woman writer / by Karen Desrosiers...[et al.].
p.   cm.
Includes bibliographical references and index.
ISBN 1-58654-028-9
1. Authorship—Collaboration. 2. Women and literature. I.
Desrosiers, Karen, 1963-
PN145.G76   2003
808'.02'082—dc21

2 0 0 2 1 5 5 2 0 1

Book Design by Lisa Garbutt

To our families
who gave us
love,
support,
and
"a room of our own."

Acknowledgments

A cast of characters contributed to the creation of this book in many ways. Kelley Conway helped us believe in ourselves as writers in her creative writing workshops. This is an important scene in our story—it's where we met!

Barbara Benham and Martha Walsh, our two other group members, are integral parts of our writing group who had other commitments that prevented them from working as authors on this project. Their contribution as group members is evident in the examples given in this book.

Thank you, Cyndy Benoit and Martha Walsh, for being readers of the manuscript. Our gratitude goes to Laurel Lloyd Earnshaw for the extra hours she devoted to prepare the manuscript for submission.

We would also like to thank our families, who have made many sacrifices so that we could work on this project together, and our friends, who listen to, encourage, and support our love of writing. The New Hampshire Writer's Project, our state writers' organization, has provided us with resources that educate and conference days that stimulate. And finally, we thank Robert McDowell and the staff of Story Line Press for their belief in our book and for providing the opportunity to reach other women writers.

CONTENTS

PART TWO: GROUP IMPACT ON CRAFT

PART THREE: RESOURCES

"I wanted to encourage the young women."

VIRGINIA WOOLF, explaining to a friend why she
wrote the 1929 book, *A Room of One's Own*

"Women's writing has...been impoverished by
the limited access women have had to life....Yet
the hiddenness, the anonymity of women's lives
has endowed them with a great beauty, and the
challenge Woolf gives to women writers is to
capture these lives in all their variety."

MARY GORDON, Preface, *A Room of One's Own*

INTRODUCTION

Can a women's writing group save your marriage, improve your sex life, and help you lose twenty pounds? Okay, so maybe we don't have the miracle cure for all of life's desires, but we do know a way you can achieve your writing dreams whether you're an accomplished writer or a beginner. The secret resides within the pages of this book—brought to you courtesy of the Southern New Hampshire Women's Writing Group.

We began our journey together in 1996 and had such an adventure that we wanted to share our experience with you. To say that the writing group has instilled fun into our lives is an understatement. It has brought camaraderie, support, and validation—all while propelling our individual writing to new heights. The nurturing environment of a women's writing group can do the same for you.

Virginia Woolf encouraged women to create "a room of their own" to explore their creative lives. In today's fast-paced world where time is at a minimum, women need more than physical space and the financial means to realize their artistic passions. They need time and a path. In *A Group of One's Own: Nurturing the Woman Writer*, we show you a path. You may decide to join a group already in existence or create a group of your own. Regardless of your approach, the end result will be the same: joining forces with like-minded women will make your journey a memorable and productive one.

There are many ways to venture on a journey. Before the creation of our writing group, we traveled alone, having no sense of what a group could offer us collectively. After the group took shape, the synergy of our individual talents produced a dynamic that took us to places we never expected to visit, including the development of this book.

A Group Of One's Own: Nurturing the Woman Writer is divided into three main sections:

- **Part One** describes how to create a nurturing group environment that enables all participants to excel in their writing. Intermixed with the details of creating and running a group are tips about providing constructive feedback to others, finding the time to write, organizing artist dates and retreats, and getting your work published.

- **Part Two** includes samples of work from the members of the group, with each author explaining how the group affected the development of her piece.

- **Part Three** provides resources to help you get started on your writing journey, such as web sites, examples of our group documents, and marketing materials. We've also included some of our favorite books.

We believe that belonging to a group of your own will help you reach your personal writing goals. There is power in joining forces with other women. In *A Group of One's Own: Nurturing the Woman Writer*, we will take you on a journey where you will never be alone. Please join us, and we will travel together, arm-in-arm.

Seth Wereska

From left, Laurel Lloyd Earnshaw, Deborah Regan, Susan Wereska,
Karen Desrosiers, and Charlene Pollano

PART ONE

The Journey

One

WHY A WRITING GROUP?

The Southern New Hampshire Women's Writing Group (SNHWWG) had no pre-conceived notion about how to create or run a group when we first started meeting in 1996. Rather, we were individuals from a variety of backgrounds who wanted to make writing an important part of our lives. Most of us had met at a workshop and, when it ended, wanted to continue writing. We began meeting at a local McDonald's restaurant to share our work. There were three of us then—Charlene, Sue, and Martha. One year later Laurel joined the group, soon followed by Barbara, Deborah, and Karen.

Without a map to lead us on our journey, we focused on moving in a direction that would allow us to explore our creativity. Several years after joining forces, we realized we had surpassed both our individual and group expectations. As we looked back on where we had traveled, we questioned what had enabled us to flourish and, more importantly, how we could share our knowledge with other aspiring authors so they, too, could realize their dreams. Our discussion about this topic inspired us to create this book.

When we first started meeting, not all of us had been published, but that quickly changed as our skills improved. Today we've been published in academic journals, magazines, newspapers, books, and through public radio and Internet publications. The nurturing environment of the group, combined with hard work and dedication, made it all possible. It can happen for you, too, regardless of where you are on your journey.

Do any of these scenarios apply to you?

- *You dream about being a writer and have no idea where to start.*

- *You had a bad experience when sharing your writing and stopped writing as a result.*

- *You like to write but have no place to share your work.*

- *You feel your writing would benefit from constructive feedback.*

- *When writing, you feel isolated or lonely.*

- *You'd like to meet others who share your writing interest.*

- *You'd like to try different types of writing.*

- *You want ideas about getting your work published.*

If you answered yes, we have some ideas for you! We experienced these situations in various ways and used the strength of the writing group to move on. There is a group out there that will propel you toward your writing goals. If you can't find one, you can create a group of your own—like we did. We've written this book to show you how.

Here are some of the immediate benefits you will receive from a group of your own.

1. A Built-in Support Network—Being with a group of like-minded individuals who know what it's like to face a blank page or to get the dreaded rejection letter in the mail can be the glue that holds a writer together. We should know—we've nearly set the Guinness Record for Coming Unglued. No matter what difficulty you're experiencing in your writing career—be it frustration, intimidation, or writer's block—a built-in support network will make your journey smoother.

2. Validation—When you join a writing group, the family and friends who previously viewed your writing as a frivolous hobby will realize you are serious. Perhaps you hadn't been taking yourself seriously. Being part of a group involves commitments and responsibilities to others. You will need to carve time out of your busy life to write and, depending on the format of your group, to critique the work of others. Joining forces with others validates your quest.

*3. Nurturing Environment—*Women are born nurturers. They know just what to say when you're overwhelmed with life—not to mention the writing project you intended to tackle last week. A writing group will soothe your weary soul when you need it most or, at a minimum, suggest you soak in a hot tub or go for a walk to get back on course.

*4. Constructive Feedback—*So you've been writing, but you have no idea if your story has achieved its intended effect. Perhaps a story gets rejected by an editor or publisher, and you can't figure out why. Regardless of the particulars, a writing group functions as a team of editors. You can get objective feedback about your work so you don't have to write in a creative vacuum.

*5. Increased Productivity—*There's nothing like a deadline to get the creative juices flowing. When participating in a writing group, it's inevitable that you will be writing more since you'll probably have deadlines. Suddenly you need to make time to write instead of hoping words will miraculously appear on the blank page. The pages accumulate and you are on your way.

*6. Shared Ideas and Networking—*Group members share ideas and tips that can move your writing forward. Maybe you need input on getting a piece published or are looking for a detail in a story to make it complete. When you're part of a writing group, you have a wealth of information and ideas at your fingertips.

Regardless of your current relationship to writing, it's never too late to begin a new adventure. It's a matter of taking that first step.

why all women?

Years ago, before women entered the workforce, there were church groups, sewing bees, and coffee klatches—all reasons for women to come together to share their skills and energy (and perhaps a small amount of gossip). Today, women are often isolated from each other, rushing to jobs and keeping family commitments—with no time for community. Many are in search of a forum to meet and bond with others like themselves. Oprah's Book Club was a wonderful example of how women found common ground to come together to read, discuss, and share literature. Writing groups are a natural outgrowth of that love of literature as we take the love of the written word to another level.

Author Elizabeth Berg says, "There are groups that are all one sex; and there are those that are mixed. I have been in both and find that although a man's point of view is of great value, I prefer, and tend to profit more from, all-women groups."

We didn't set out to be an all-women's group, yet the dynamic has been an ideal fit for all the members. Here are some reasons why.

Karen says, "Writing is such a personal vocation—I put my heart, soul, and most intimate secrets on the page, often only thinly disguised. It's hard enough to get used to and overcome the fear of exposure; having men in the group would prompt me to censor myself far more than I do otherwise."

Charlene adds, "Our group is made up of very strong, independent women. We all have interests in women's issues. Not that this would preclude men from being members, rather it's a common thread that runs throughout. The SNHWWG evolved from an all women's writing workshop and continued from there. It works, and why mess with success? Would the dynamics change if a man entered the inner sanctum? Probably."

Sue says that she likes the company of men and respects their opinions, but science has proven that men and women think and see the world differently. "There is a basis of understanding formed by prior biological and cultural experiences. I believe there are two advantages to having a group made up exclusively of women. First, what a woman brings to the page means she will read the message differently than a man. Second, the feedback a woman receives from women will be different because they tend to recognize the value of relationship building more."

will you join us?

We began our journey as writers without a map, but we had the fortune to cross paths. Since forming the group, we haven't looked back; our eyes are fixed on the horizon.

Are you looking for a path? We have uncovered one to writing that will offer you the adventure of a lifetime, and we're here to share it with you.

Two

(O)PENING LINES

If we've managed to convince you that being part of a writing group is the best thing since computers replaced pens, you'll be wondering how to join or start a writing group.

The first question to ask yourself is whether you want to join an existing group or create your own. Your decision will depend on the level of effort you want to expend as well as the resources available to you. Creating your own group takes more time, but you will have more influence in shaping the group to meet your needs.

joining an existing group

Initially, joining an existing writing group may be easier than starting one on your own unless you already have some dedicated writing friends who want to accompany you on your journey. There are several ways to locate a writing group which involve connecting with other writers.

▨ FINDING OTHER WRITERS

If you are a novice or intermediate writer, one option is to take writing workshops, conferences, or classes. You could ask your writing instructor if she or he knows of any existing groups. Once you've had an opportunity to get to know your fellow classmates, seek out those with whom you share a common feedback style and whose writing skill you admire. Ask if they are currently part of a writing group, and if they are, whether there are any openings for new members. If they aren't part of a group, and they would also like to join one, you can search together.

Writing courses and workshops can be found at colleges and universities, adult education programs, women's groups, and writing organizations. Your local library and bookstore may have information on writing groups as well.

Writing conferences can provide an opportunity for individual writers to read their work out loud, also called open mike readings. These readings are also offered at bookstores and libraries. If you can muster the courage to do this—not for the faint of heart, but it can boost your writing ego—other writers may approach you afterward to discuss your work. This discussion can lead to the topic of writing groups. Some workshop presenters are members of writing groups or offer writing workshops themselves.

STATE AND NATIONAL RESOURCES

Local and national resources may also provide a way to meet other writers. Your state may have an existing organization for writers that can be found by contacting the state council on the arts. The New Hampshire Writer's Project (NHWP) has a newsletter and web page that include information about writing groups that are open to new members. In addition, the NHWP offers workshops and an annual writing conference, all of which are great places to meet writers. Your local newspaper or community website may also list writing conferences.

Publications such as *Poets and Writers* and *Writer's Digest* offer information about writing workshops and conferences. Some, such as the prestigious Bread Loaf Writer's Conference in Vermont or the University of Iowa Writer's Conference, are designed for advanced writers. Many others are appropriate for intermediate or beginning writers.

The Writer's Center in Maryland offers over 240 workshops each year and lists over 40 literary centers around the country. Their website can be found in Part Three. These non-profit groups provide such services as writing workshops, newsletters, writer workspace, and equipment. Many of the literary centers use names that reflect their geographic location, and all are listed alphabetically by the name of the center.

Whether you choose a state or national organization, a writer's magazine, or a conference, you will soon find that writers are everywhere!

FINDING A GROUP THE LOW TECH WAY

If you are unable to find writing groups or courses in your area, a radical approach may be needed. Seek out a local bookstore, preferably the type that is furnished with comfy sofas and chairs where people spend hours perusing the shelves. Pull up a chair next to the shelves in the writing section, select a couple of books and wait. After someone strolls into your section and begins to search for a book on writing, ask them if they've read any of the ones you have selected. If a conversation on writing ensues, ask if they write, what they write, and if they know of or are part of a writing group. And, hey, if you don't meet a writing group, you may meet the partner of your dreams!

FINDING A GROUP THE HIGH TECH WAY

The Internet is a great resource though less cozy than your local bookstore. Writing groups and organizations abound on the Internet, some specific to genres of writing, like Horror Writers and Romance Writers. A search on the keywords "writing groups" produced over 21 million responses, and even when narrowing it down to "writing groups—New Hampshire," the list was over 16 million. Since many of the websites listed may not meet your needs, you will need to be more specific in your search. *Poets and Writers* magazine has a website that often shares ads for writing groups. Part Three lists some of our favorite websites.

what to look for in a group

Once you've found a group, don't rest on your literary sleuthing laurels yet. You may have found a group, but have you found the ideal writing group for your needs?

Elizabeth Berg says, "What I look for in a writing group member is good writing, honesty, intelligence, sensitivity, a good sense of humor, and fine cooking skills. Not necessarily in that order. Perhaps most important, a good group member is that most old-fashioned and wonderful of things: kind. That means she has an ability and willingness to be careful not only with another writer's words, but with that person's heart."

▨ WRITING GENRE

Consider whether the writing genre of the group members fits with your primary genre, and if not, whether that is important to you. If you are a novelist, for example, are many of the group members also novelists? Writers who write poetry, essays, fiction and non-fiction are all equally adept at providing feedback, but will they know your literary form as well as their own? Many fiction writers may benefit from the specific word choice and rhythm that a poet can provide as feedback. However, fiction writers often find it difficult to provide pertinent feedback on poetry, if they are unaccustomed to that genre.

▨ COMMITMENT

> "Writers can be a unique breed of people, living frequently in make-believe worlds of their own creation. The writing group provides me with a community."—Karen

If you are serious about writing, find a group of people who are also serious and willing to commit time and energy to the group. If you are just beginning to explore writing and are more interested in camaraderie, look for a group that is more casual. Also, find a group whose schedule fits your needs. If the group gives feedback to all members at every meeting and you aren't able to do that much work, it may not be the right group for you. On the other hand, if you want feedback at least once a month, make sure the schedule can accommodate you.

▨ DEMOGRAPHICS

Consider whether other demographics are important to you, such as age, gender, and the writing experience of the members. In the Southern New Hampshire Women's Writing Group, we enjoy and benefit from a diversity of age, occupation, and background. Although the demographics of group members may be irrelevant, their dedication to writing should be consistent.

▨ STYLES OF FEEDBACK

A crucial detail to consider in a group is the manner in which feedback is provided. In Chapter 4 we discuss our philosophy on feedback. When joining a group, it is appropriate to ask members to discuss their feedback style, and then observe them in action to determine if the actual practice follows the philosophy. Beware of the group that claims they are supportive when, in practice, the fangs and claws appear as they tear into each other's work like hungry hyenas.

Some of the SNHWWG members have participated in writing workshops in which virtually all of the feedback a writer received was negative. Given in such a manner, many writers felt hurt and humiliated. This method of providing feedback is particularly damaging and could prevent a talented writer from continuing to pursue her craft. This is unfortunate for the individual writer and her potential audience as one more woman's voice is silenced.

Ultimately, the group's feedback on your writing is going to have the greatest impact on your self-confidence as a writer. A writer who is encouraged is more likely to continue to write and, after all, isn't that the primary goal? Generally, if a writer feels as though feedback is provided in a caring, supportive, and non-judgmental manner, she will be more inclined to incorporate that feedback in her work. That said, a group that provides only positive feedback might make you feel good about your writing but not help you to improve your skills.

PURPOSE OF THE GROUP

Before deciding whether to commit to your new group, ask about their purpose. While our group has a specific format and purpose, there are others that function quite differently. Some offer a forum for writers to read their work aloud, after which they give exclusively positive feedback to the writer. Their objective is to provide writers with an opportunity to hear their work, gain the experience of reading in front of a group, and increase their self-esteem. Our group includes the option to read aloud. Others have improving writing skills as their primary purpose, or a focus on increasing creativity, or sharing tips about getting published.

Some groups actually write together during their sessions, often in the form of freewriting, for a specific amount of time. When they finish, each writer reads her work aloud, and afterwards, each member comments on the piece. At the conclusion of the writing exercise, the group discusses general writing issues, often brought up by topics from the discussion.

Initially you may want to ask your prospective group if you can observe for a session or two before making a commitment to join, like Cyndy Benoit did in our group. Requesting a trial membership may help you determine if the group is right for you. Joining a group on a trial basis may allow you to observe and then gracefully withdraw from the group if it doesn't meet your needs. Look at the give and take. Whether you observe or try on the group, ask yourself if you meet the requirements of the group, such as providing feedback, attending meetings, and writing.

growing a group

If you have been unable to find an existing writing group and have decided to form one yourself, begin by examining some of the details regarding writing genre, commitment, demographics, and feedback. Envision the perfect writing group as your destination, and then take the first step of your journey. Who knows what adventures and challenges you will find along the way?

Do you know any other writers you could enlist in your group who could help you find other members? What resources can you use to advertise your group? Many of the resources for finding a group, such as a writing course, conference, or statewide writing organization, can be used to advertise your group. Instead of attending a reading, perhaps you and another co-founder of your group could provide a reading at a local library or bookstore. You could try advertising on the website of an existing writer's organization or even create your own website. Other options include placing a notice in the newspaper or posting one on the bulletin board of your local library, bookstore, or grocery store.

WHAT'S IN A NAME?

At some point, you may want to give your group a name. The name can be reflective of your geographic location and gender of your group like ours (Southern New Hampshire Women's Writing Group), the writing genre of your group (Murderous Mystery Writers), when your group meets (Occasional Tuesday Night Group), or something that reflects your group goals (We Are Going to Get Published Someday Writing Group!). A name can make your venture seem more official.

WE ARE FAMILY

While exploring the opportunity to create or get adopted into the ideal writing family, be certain that the group shares a common approach to writing. You'll hopefully be spending a lot of time together over the upcoming years, so you want to be part of a positive, nurturing environment. Is the group inclusive of all members' needs when developing a schedule? Do all members use the feedback style and format defined by the group? Do they have well developed guidelines for feedback and submission of work? Are they supportive of each other's work? Is their intent to help others be the best writers they can be?

let the adventure begin!

Whether you choose to join an existing writing group or form one of your own, there are many resources available to help you take this first step toward ensuring that writing becomes a permanent and rewarding part of your life. We've offered some tips to get you started. So what are you waiting for?

Three

Managing the Details

Does your writing group discuss what they've been reading, movies they've seen, the state of the union, and only occasionally find time to review a member's work? That's great—if it serves everyone's needs. However, if your writing group intends to help members further themselves as writers, grow their craft, and chase the elusive dream of being published, this may not be so straightforward. Many details go into forming and maintaining an effective writing group, just like any other group. Keeping the group together and turning it into a functioning, successful entity that meets the writing needs of its members is another thing altogether.

The bottom line is that if your group is going to thrive, it needs some attention—some tender and some tough love.

bigger isn't always better

Does size really matter? Let's be honest, regardless of the context of this question, few would answer "no." Your waistline, your house, your diamond, your salary, your…well, you get the picture. It applies to nearly every other aspect of our lives, and it applies to writing groups.

You've spent time looking for the right group. Perhaps you followed some of our suggestions in Chapter 2. Just as important as the right group is the size of the group. A writing group needs intimacy to be effective—something a cast-of-thousands, or even twenty, couldn't provide. It also needs to be manageable and provide equal time and space to all of its members, at a frequency that is acceptable to everyone. Is it going to meet your needs if the size of the group dictates that you only receive feedback twice a year? Then again, if your group is so small you are expected to submit every week, you may not be able to keep up the pace.

The optimal size varies from one to another depending on the type and structure of the group, which may range in size from four to twelve members. In the Southern New Hampshire Women's Writing Group, we have a limit of eight members.

determining the logistics

A primary task for any writing group is to set a schedule, deciding on where, when, how long, and how often to meet.

First, let's look at where. The choices will depend on what's available. Some locations we've tried are restaurants, libraries, members' homes, and bookstores. Take into consideration distractions, noise level, and equitable driving distances for all members. The distance that members live from the site of the group meeting may impact their attendance. Our members live up to a one hour drive from one another. Restaurants are convenient if you meet around dinner time, and members' homes are ideal if you, or the restaurant, tend to get loud. You may also want to be aware of the topics you will be discussing and their appropriateness for the meeting location. We once found ourselves discussing an x-rated scene from a member's story in the middle of a family restaurant and whispered our way through feedback.

When, how long, and how often you meet are dependent on the schedules and needs of members and the purpose of your group. Some groups gather anywhere from weekly to monthly, from one hour to several, on any day of the week. Coming up with a schedule that works for all members of the group may be one of your hardest tasks. Spend some time on this, and do everything possible to keep it consistent. If coming up with a schedule is hard, adjusting it can be harder.

The members of the SNHWWG have found that meeting every two to three weeks, at six or seven in the evening, for two hours, works ideally for us. We vary the location of our meetings to keep the commute time fair for all members. In the summer we often schedule meetings farther apart to accommodate busy lives, and we usually take December off (except, of course, for our annual Christmas extravaganza).

setting dates and agendas

Because we vary the location, and our starting time often depends on the closing time of the venue, we schedule our meetings in three month blocks. When we set the dates of our meetings, we also determine who will receive feedback. Meetings are structured to give each member three opportunities for feedback per calendar quarter. We agree on our meeting nights, determine the schedule, and choose our feedback slots. The written schedule includes who should be submitting and receiving feedback for any given meeting. Developing a schedule also enables us to plan around holidays and vacations. Not all members can attend all meetings. Knowing this in advance allows us to plan ahead.

Generally the agenda of a meeting is the same from one to the next and follows the purpose of the group. If your writing group focuses on giving feedback, the agenda will need feedback time slots. However, there may be other issues that also need to be discussed, such as setting goals or reviewing materials from workshops. It is a good idea to build these items into the meeting agenda to have enough time for both discussion and scheduled feedback.

For the SNHWWG, a typical meeting agenda consists of three feedback slots. We generally spend a few minutes catching up and sharing news before getting down to business. The remaining time is divided equally among the three members receiving feedback, taking short breaks in between. We devote thirty minutes to each author's work.

Of course there are groups that don't go through as much effort as we do to develop schedules and plan meetings. Some may like a more spontaneous approach, deciding on meeting times from one to the next, and providing feedback to whomever is ready, when they're ready.

who's running the show?

As you will see throughout this book, writing groups come in many sizes and shapes. Some have clear leaders and some are free-for-alls. The decision about whether to have a group leader is one that all members of the group must agree on and be comfortable with.

Having a leader means there is someone who manages details such as watching the time and maintaining the schedules. However, having one person who manages the group on a permanent basis does not lend itself to equality among members.

Allowing the group to run in a less structured way can be more conducive to the creative process. Feedback can spawn discussion, which can lead to brainstorming and major breakthroughs for a writer who may be struggling. And, of course, there are more opportunities to socialize. Unfortunately, it is unlikely that everyone will receive the same amount of time for feedback, and it is possible that someone may miss her feedback altogether.

Laurel shares an experience from a writing workshop where there was no clear leader. "One individual spent so much time talking about her own work that other participants didn't have time to share theirs. I felt bad for the women who took the workshop solely to find an audience for their own work because they lost that opportunity. Had an instructor limited the domineering person's style or given each participant an equal amount of time to present her work, the workshop would have been more balanced."

Dr. Allan Lefcowitz of The Writer's Center recommends that each critique session have a different leader and that the leader should not be receiving feedback on that night. He explains that the leader's task is to keep discussions focused and on time.

At the outset we operated our meetings on an honor system. We loosely tried to monitor the time and ensure equitable feedback while having no designated leader. This worked to some degree because we have strong feedback guidelines. However, we frequently went off on tangents and lost track of our purpose. This resulted in the final member's feedback time being shorter than the others'.

Later we devised the idea of a rotating facilitator where each meeting would have a designated leader. The facilitator has a number of responsibilities including monitoring time to ensure that everyone has the same amount of time for feedback. She also takes and distributes meeting notes and is the central contact for anyone who is unable to attend a meeting. We volunteer as meeting facilitators when we set up the schedule. Each member chooses to moderate a meeting when she will not be receiving feedback.

On our quarterly schedule form, we include the date, time, and location of the meeting, who is submitting and receiving feedback, and the facilitator.

taking it one step farther

Once you have a working group, you may be content leaving well enough alone. You may want to make the group stronger, assist each other on a deeper level, or move closer to a more business-like working entity. There are a number of ways that the group can grow and develop.

GOAL SETTING

Writers, especially those intent on writing seriously, should set realistic goals for themselves, even though this is not an easy task. If done within the writing group, members can help each other define attainable goals, inject reality checks when necessary, encourage goals that further each member's writing, and introduce challenges along the way. A goal might be as specific as submitting a piece to a particular publication or as broad as writing every day.

How often you set goals as a group will depend on the group's desires and needs. While some people prefer quarterly goals, others may prefer to set them monthly, semi-annually, or annually. It is important to review the goals regularly. Reviewing them allows the individual writer to track her progress and identify problems with her writing process. This also allows the group to celebrate accomplishments, and we're always looking for a reason to celebrate!

The members of the SNHWWG set goals for three months at a time. At the same meeting we review our previous goals, set new ones, and prepare the feedback schedule. There is resounding applause and cheers when a member accomplishes her stated goals for a time-period.

MISSION STATEMENTS

A mission statement is a useful tool to help writers focus on long-range goals for both the group and individual. In the SNHWWG we encourage each writer to develop a mission statement regarding her own writing ambitions and help each other keep them reasonable and realistic. We have also worked together to define a mission statement for the group itself. (See Part Three for examples.)

Sue says, "I find security in knowing that all of the members believe our purpose is to encourage women to write and publish. That frees me to be more creative when I write. The discussions we had in formulating our mission statement also helped me to develop a sense of security for sharing my first draft work. Often it's in that first messy tilling of the soil that the seeds of creative ideas are found."

"Having a mission statement helps our group stay focused."
—Sue

EXPECTATIONS AND GUIDELINES

Group expectations and guidelines should be defined up front to ensure that the writing group functions smoothly. These should be documented and made available to each member to serve as the covenants for the group. New members should receive this information, as well as the group mission statement, when deciding whether to join the group.

> "Hell, there are no rules here—we're just trying to accomplish something."
> —Thomas A. Edison

So what policies do you need for a writing group? It is, as always, ultimately dependent on the members and purpose of your group. A more social, casual group will have fewer expectations than a serious, goal-oriented group. The following is a sample of items you may want to discuss and document in your group guidelines:

- *Attendance expectations*

- *Membership commitment*

- *Feedback and submissions*

- *Policies for admitting new members*

- *Group structure and operations*

- *Methods of problem resolution*

ROOM FOR NEW MEMBERS

If you've already decided on a membership limit, you will know when you are open to new members. Perhaps you've decided to increase the size of your group and bring in new blood. If you're ready to bring new members into the fold, there are a few considerations to discuss.

Adding one stop along your route can change the experience entirely. Likewise, adding a new member to the group can completely change the group's dynamics. If it's a good match, the change can enhance the group. If not a good one, it can have serious repercussions for existing members.

Should you decide to admit new members into the group, the SNHWWG has two suggestions. First, have written materials available for the new member. These will help her to become familiar with the group's process, how feedback works, and other group standards. Second, set up an observation phase so that a potential new member can try out the group while the group tries out the new member.

Some groups screen potential new members. This can be done by having the writer submit samples of her work for the group to review before final acceptance to determine that writing skills are comparable. You may also want to consider what genre she writes.

TAKING STOCK

Set times to step back and review your progress. Is your group moving forward? Are the members growing as writers? Ensure that the schedule is still effective. Set aside a meeting during which everyone can voice ideas and concerns. Talk about which aspects of the group are working and which may need revision. Communication is the grease that keeps the wheels rolling along our journey.

getting lost along the way

Groups progress through a series of developmental phases much like relationships. Orientation, hesitant participation, and search for meaning are characteristic of all new relationships—each member getting to know each other and attempting to find common ground. As the relationship grows, members may enter a period of conflict, dominance, and rebellion. Finally the relationship will reach cohesion, during which morale, trust, and self-disclosure increase dramatically.

These stages can be seen in a writing group through a variety of situations and behaviors. For the SNHWWG the first phase was marked with meetings in a busy McDonald's and members' anxiety over revealing too much of themselves through their writing. There was also a level of questioning and fear surrounding feedback as we learned to trust and honor each other. The second phase arrived as the group was beginning to feel comfortable with each other. Attendance began to decline and some members weren't regularly submitting work for feedback. Resentments began to grow. The SNHWWG began moving into the third stage of group dynamics as we learned to voice our concerns, identify our goals and expectations, and find our way to publication. Our morale, intimacy, and trust grew, showing in our writing with increased courage and conviction.

All good relationships will experience problems from time to time. No group, even one for the purpose of writing, can go forever without encountering rough waters. Occasionally things go awry, but most of the time everything will be smooth, the group will be effective, and its members will be happy and successful.

ANOTHER LOOK AT THE MAP

First and foremost, if you haven't defined the expectations and guidelines for the group as discussed above, now is the time to do it. Stopping to ask directions isn't the most efficient approach, but it's better than ending up in the wrong country.

When the SNHWWG began experiencing problems with participation and commitment, we held a meeting to define guidelines for the group. It was this process of addressing the issues and defining some ground-rules that enabled us to move from mild tension to cohesion.

COMMUNICATION IS KEY TO SUCCESS

Since a writing group is no different than any other group or interpersonal relationship, people will disagree from time to time. A group member may assume a leadership role while other members would rather not have a leader at all. Feedback may be harsh, insensitive, or inadequate. A group member may take over, interrupt the feedback, and monopolize discussions.

We have found that when problems do arise, it's best to bring them out in the open rather than keep them bottled up. Of course, it is also best to approach all problems with diplomacy and sensitivity. But we're talking about women, right? We're good at sensitivity, but confrontation may be more challenging.

At difficult times, issues should be handled through a process of discussion, consensus building, and compromise until an agreement can be reached. It's beneficial to bring an issue out into the open so that tensions don't build. If necessary, a group may also consider bringing in an outside mediator to assist in problem resolution. This can be easier if you build the format for discussing concerns into the group agenda, such as setting aside time at a quarterly meeting. It is important to keep the group focused and keep the lines of communication open.

CREATIVE SOLUTIONS TO SOME COMMON PROBLEMS

What do you do when a member of the group is not writing regularly, submitting to the group, providing feedback on other members' work, or attending meetings? How much these issues matter depends on the purpose and commitment of your writing group.

In our group, it is a serious matter if someone repeatedly does not submit writing for feedback as scheduled. Not doing so leaves a feedback slot open at the meeting—a third of the meeting with nothing scheduled. That's also a feedback slot someone else could have used if she had known it was available.

Whenever a member is failing to meet the expectations and commitments outlined for the group, the other members should approach her in a sensitive and concerned way. The group should come to an agreement and address the member together. The question then becomes how to handle the problem.

For members who are unable to meet the expectations and workload, we have adopted a policy of second chances. If the group has approached a member regarding her level of participation, it is with the intent of giving her a second chance. However, the group will have to decide how many second chances can be extended to a member.

If the member is unable to meet the guidelines for a period of time but does not want to leave the group entirely, a sabbatical provides the perfect solution. A member may also need to take a break from the group due to scheduling conflicts or for personal reasons such as family, work, or illness. In this way, a member is able to take a break without disrupting the functioning of the entire group. A sabbatical also provides the opportunity to invite a temporary member into the group, as we did with Susanne Whayne.

WHEN IT'S THE WRONG FIT

No matter how hard we try to make it all work, it's not always possible. Each member must make the decisions that work best for her and her craft. You may want to consider trying on several groups until you find the best fit. Clarifying your expectations, needs, and goals will help you narrow the search for the right group.

It is hard to start over, to give up the trust and comfort already developed. To break ties and move toward the unknown may be the only answer. Be honest with yourself and your group. If the group isn't working for you, it may be time to find a new group of your own.

the meeting is adjourned

Like most other situations, the more work you put into your group, the more effective it will be in the long run. Once the group has been organized and the ground-rules laid, issues may arise. The better prepared you are, the better you will survive the hard times. Take some time to review goals, procedures, and communications with your group. If all the components are in place, the result will be a personal win for your own writing and a collective win for your writing group.

Four

EVERYTHING YOU NEED TO KNOW ABOUT FEEDBACK

What do you think of when someone mentions feedback? Is it your boss's opinion of your job performance? Perhaps it's information about your progress at the gym. Maybe it's that horrible screeching sound your son's stereo equipment makes!

If you're a writer, feedback is the opportunity to receive input from group members about a piece of your writing. It's exciting, challenging, and it can be scary. You dread it because it leaves you feeling vulnerable, and you know it will result in more work. At the same time, you look forward to it because you know it helps to sharpen your writing skills as nothing else can.

Feedback is a way to measure how close a writer comes to communicating her intended message. Because the act of writing is private and solitary, there is always a risk that an author's words will be misunderstood, will create unwanted controversy, or perhaps even offend. With practice, the author learns how to use words to affect an audience.

"My work has been heard into existence by other women"
— Susan Griffin

ways to get feedback

Just as there are many routes to get to a destination, there are many ways to obtain feedback on your writing. One of the easiest ways is to ask friends to read your work, as author Stephen King does. After his wife reads his manuscript, he sends it to several other people to read before submitting to his publisher.

Some people seek help on the Internet. If you decide to try this, thinking that you will find a site to critique your work, good luck! Many of the college sites offer guidelines stating their expectations for students' written work. Others feature private individuals, working as consultants, who expect payment for editing services. If you are lucky, you will find an on-line writing group that may be willing to look at your work because they want to support a potential author. If you are not lucky, there will be a fee.

Taking a writing course where an author expects to be evaluated is another form of feedback. Deborah tells about an experience that almost ended her career as a writer. "Most of the feedback I received on my writing throughout elementary and high school was very positive. That changed when I took a creative writing course taught by a well known writer in college. He told me that my writing was trite and needed to be grittier. The critical feedback was damaging enough to my self-esteem as a writer that I didn't write for fifteen years. I could scream now to think of the time I wasted when I could have been developing my craft."

Sue's experience as a participant in the Writing Process Summer Institute at the University of New Hampshire (UNH) was just the opposite. Students met with well known authors who discussed their own writing process and talked about the types of problems writers face and how they were able to cope. Student authors were divided into small groups where they were given the opportunity to share their writing. Guidelines were designed to both encourage and protect the novice writers. These authors read their work orally while individual members of the audience prepared written feedback. The comments were required to include praise for the elements of writing that were done well and questions to help the writers determine where more work was needed.

Author Maya Angelou wrote about the first time she received feedback in a writing group. As each member's work was critiqued, it was torn to shreds. Although Angelou believes she's a stronger writer as a result, many women would not have persevered.

Over a period of several years, members of the Southern New Hampshire Women's Writing Group took workshops taught by a local author whose approach to feedback was similar to the one used at UNH and other colleges. The process included beginning with encouraging comments and telling what we, as readers, wanted more of or didn't understand. This style of feedback formed a solid foundation that enabled the group to trust one another. As our group developed, we further refined our feedback approach.

The women in the SNHWWG have found, through experience, that feedback is best received in a safe and intimate setting, and when it is given by other writers. How many writers have put the pen down because they received negative feedback from someone who did not understand what it is like to be a writer? Almost every author has experienced showing a piece of work to a friend or family member, only to feel misunderstood and discouraged by the resulting comments. A writing group provides an ongoing opportunity to receive feedback from writers you know and trust.

> "Feedback is a bittersweet experience. You look forward to it and dread it at the same time."—Sue

types of feedback

A basic principle of art—that form follows function—also applies to the way a writing group gives feedback. Each group will develop a different method based on its goals. Some groups do not allow the author to speak at all while receiving feedback. Others give only negative feedback, while some groups allow only positive comments. Some groups do not require authors to submit their work ahead of time, and they respond orally as the piece is read.

The members of the SNHWWG decided early on that it is important to be sensitive to where the writer is in her writing process. Our purpose is to encourage the writer to keep writing, to believe in herself as a writer, and to develop her skills as she tells her story.

> "I joined a writing group as a way to further my craft, improve my writing, and move closer to completing and publishing projects. I wanted to find people who could give me knowledgeable, subjective, and objective input on my work."—Karen

As group members tried writing a variety of genres over the years, we found a need to have several types of feedback available. When we write first drafts, we often request that readers focus on the big picture: organization, setting, pace, plot, believability, and character development. Later drafts often need dialogue revision, details, showing versus telling, foreshadowing, and flashbacks. Authors often request that readers look for places to add or delete information to expand or shorten scenes. Final drafts require line edits for grammar, spelling, and language use. Members indicate the type of feedback they would like when they submit their work.

In our group, feedback is generally given in a round robin format, where members take turns discussing the author's work, always beginning with its strengths. Clarifying questions and constructive criticism follow. Each reader is allowed three to five minutes to respond to the writing. The time limit ensures that everyone who is scheduled for feedback will have time to be critiqued. One of the reasons we decided to cap our membership at eight members was to give us more time for feedback. During this time the author remains silent, except to occasionally answer questions that will enhance the critique being given. This approach moves the feedback along and prevents discussions that could become defensive or counterproductive.

Each reader supplements her oral comments with a one page written response. It is not always possible to do revision work immediately after receiving feedback, and important comments may be forgotten without the written portion. New ideas often result from rereading feedback, especially when enough time has passed to give the writer some distance from the piece. It is also helpful to read encouraging comments when faced with writer's block or the discouragement of a publisher's rejection.

Discussion often continues between the feedback slots. Many times members give each other tips on potential publishing markets. Ideas for crazy plot twists and strategies for changing characters often result in even more creative ideas for the author to bring home.

Another type of feedback that a member may request is to read her piece to the group and then listen to open discussion. Sometimes the writer will choose to have another member read for her so that she can listen as well. If the author has been struggling with a writing problem, the sessions often focus on brainstorming ideas to help her solve it. In the best sessions, creative ideas fly around like snowflakes in a nor'easter, with true synergy resulting in artful innovations.

When an author would like readers to take a more in-depth look at her manuscript, she can sign up for a double time slot at a regular meeting and submit up to forty pages instead of the usual twenty. For an overall look at a final draft of a novel, we schedule a month to read, then dedicate an entire evening to review the manuscript. This allows us to look closely at character consistency and at the relationship between plot points and tension. The process is rewarding for all the members because we are able to see the result of the feedback we have given on previous drafts. We read the piece like new readers and offer fresh insight. It is exciting to see a draft reach this stage in the writing process.

Feedback sessions should never become group discussions about the subject matter of the submission. For example, if the author writes about politics, the group leader should not allow the feedback session to become a forum for airing political opinions. Likewise, if the author is writing about a difficult time in her life, this is not the time for a counseling session. The leader's job is to focus comments on the goal for giving feedback: to help the writer improve and sharpen her skills and to encourage her to keep writing.

preparing for feedback

The SNHWWG members who are scheduled to receive feedback submit up to twenty typed and double spaced pages to be critiqued. These are distributed at the end of the previous meeting or sent via e-mail or snail mail at least a week to ten days before the next meeting. If a member has specific concerns or questions about her writing, she attaches a cover sheet with focus questions she would like the readers to address. These questions help the author examine whatever areas may be causing her difficulty. Outlines or summaries about previous chapters may give background information to help remind readers of the story if time has passed since feedback was last given. Additional information may include character sketches or back story.

receiving feedback

Authors need to be emotionally ready to receive feedback. Author Julia Cameron says, "Our vulnerability can feel excruciating."

Karen describes the first time she received feedback as "a very nerve-wracking experience. Just sharing my work with people was enough to give me an ulcer, but to have to hear what they thought about it, what they liked and didn't was extremely scary. I tried to emotionally disconnect as best I could and prepare myself for the onslaught. I was fortunate because I received well organized and thought provoking feedback in an extremely safe environment."

Laurel's first experience with feedback also required courage. "I felt both excited and petrified the first time I received feedback on my novel. I was excited to hear what people thought about what I had struggled to put on paper. I was also petrified that they'd feel it was junk. Looking back at the experience, I realize it was a crucial time in my development as a fiction writer. Had I received all negative feedback, I might have given up my dream to write a novel altogether."

An author needs to be able to sort through the feedback she receives, choosing to keep what enhances her vision of her story and letting the rest fall away without feeling guilty. We each must remember that we cannot please everyone, and that pleasing everyone is not the purpose of feedback.

Dr. Lefcowitz of the Writer's Center offers some good advice on this subject. "Don't argue. Don't defend. Listen. In the final analysis, it is your piece and you will benefit if the advice is useful and should not edit if the advice is not useful."

Some writers find incorporating the feedback into their revision process overwhelming. They may put it off for a while, seeking emotional distance. Others like to revise as soon as possible while the input is fresh in their minds. With practice, each writer will find her own way to incorporate feedback into her writing process.

A healthy writing group will have a feedback process that encourages the writer, while at the same time challenging her to grow and improve her writing skills. It is important to remember that we are all a work in progress. A women's writing group can provide a safe place for the fledgling writer by being sensitive to her emotional readiness to hear certain types of feedback. One way to keep members focused on this is to develop, hand out, and occasionally review printed feedback guidelines. As noted earlier, these are especially helpful for new members. It is also beneficial for a

> "If I had known in my first writing workshop that I would have to submit my writing and let it flap naked in the breeze next to eight other people, I would have turned tail and run for the hills. Once I enrolled, there was no escape. I must have turned a permanent shade of eggplant the first time I heard people talking about my writing. I've always wondered what shade I would have become if the feedback was bad!"
> —Charlene

potential member to visit a meeting or two to observe the feedback process. That way, she can decide whether she is ready to participate.

The writing group is a place for a writer to spread her wings and fly. Group members can help her mentally measure the emotional distance she has from a piece of writing by making comments and asking questions. As the writer gains confidence, she will rise to meet the challenges of her writing dream and eventually land at her intended destination.

> "This is all great feedback—the only problem is what am I going to do with it?!"
> —Deborah

benefits of feedback

No writer can look at her work objectively. Sometimes it seems like the most wonderful piece of literature ever written, and we feel a sudden urge to begin writing our acceptance speech for a Pulitzer Prize. At other times that same piece seems silly or superfluous. Getting feedback gives an author the opportunity to see her work through more objective eyes.

Karen says that feedback is a crucial part of her writing process. She depends on it to provide a sounding board. It is the first time she is able to see, hear, and experience the reaction of her audience. "For me, one of the greatest benefits of feedback is the ability to test out my work and ideas. While I may feel a particular piece is exciting, innovative, or entertaining, my opinion is extremely biased. If I receive feedback confirming my opinion, I feel good about moving forward with the piece. But if the feedback does not confirm my feelings, I know I need to go back and take a serious look at what I'm trying to say and where it's falling short."

Laurel also views feedback as an essential aspect of her work. "Without it, I'd be working in a creative vacuum. Feedback brings clarity to my work by enabling me to see what I'm communicating clearly to others and what needs to be further developed or reworked. It also gives me insight into what I'm saying; often writing group members understand what I'm trying to say before I know myself. Their feedback illuminates my direction."

Feedback also brings the experiences, knowledge, and expertise of multiple people to writing. In the SNHWWG when we have a child character, we rely on Sue, who works as a teacher. She provides a sanity check and corrects mistakes regarding child behavior and development. Martha, a software project manager, runs the numbers and tells us when things don't add up. She mentally checks our schedules and our calculations. Karen, an avid mystery reader and writer, is our resident crime expert who provides advice when our characters are in trouble with the law. Charlene, a high school counselor, knows how to up the ante when it comes to the peer pressures today's teens face. In addition, the members of our group are wives, mothers, daughters, cooks, entrepreneurs, travelers, musicians, sailors, athletes, performers, community volunteers, and political activists. When we don't know what we need to know to keep writing, we ask husbands and significant others, friends and colleagues. A writing group gives us access to a plethora of primary sources.

> "On a regular basis I receive tips from group members that help my story to be as accurate and developed as possible. Once I described a character as having teeth as big as a whale's, and Sue pointed out that most whales don't have teeth!"—Laurel

Feedback has a tremendous impact on the final product. As a result of feedback in our group, characters have been renamed, assigned new genders, married, divorced, widowed, kidnapped, and murdered. Endings have become middles, middles have become beginnings. Dialogues have been rewritten. Storms have brewed, fires have burned, cars have crashed, and international intrigue has occurred. All of this turmoil started with a simple feedback comment.

are you ready?

Does your stomach do somersaults each time you face feedback? Do you wish you had censored your entire submission? Has experience taught you that you'll go home feeling like a failure? If your answer to these questions is yes, make yourself a promise. Tell yourself that your writing is too important to subject yourself to anything less than encouragement and validation. Pledge to find a writing group that offers constructive feedback wrapped in praise. Promise that you won't settle for less when it comes to this very important aspect of writing!

Part of being a group member is giving and receiving feedback. The constructive criticism of a group informs, strengthens, and sharpens our writing. And who is the benefactor of all this? Our writing selves, of course.

Five

NURTURING INSPIRATION

How can a writing group nurture and inspire its members? A healthy writing group supplies the fertile soil for germinating and growing ideas. Although the seeds of inspiration come from within, these tender seedlings need sunshine and water to keep growing. Having thoughtful and talented peers in a writing group keeps these roots running deep.

Writing groups nurture inspiration by being supportive. Thoughts of writing keep authors together in spirit even when they are physically apart. Voices of group members echo in the writer's mind. It is easier to face the world as a writer, knowing that other women stand with you. On the days you think everything you write is kindling for the fire, there is always someone in the group who encourages you.

Author Nancy Slonim Aronie says, "...if it's really in your heart, this writing dream won't go away. It eats at you. It nudges you. It whispers in your ear until you can't ignore it any longer." In a writing group, the dream is echoed by other members who constantly remind one another that they need to do this thing called writing.

> "Strength, conviction, and support are our buttresses as we all move forward together."—Deborah

In the Southern New Hampshire Women's Writing Group, we enjoy a camaraderie that differs from long-time friendships and family connectedness, but remains steadfast and true in ways related to our common thread—writing. We discipline each other, imposing deadlines to keep focused, and we find ways to nurture our writing selves through artist dates and retreats.

affirming and encouraging one another

A good writing group supplies an endless wealth of encouragement. The writer's job lacks the customary interaction, feedback, and immediate response system available in many occupations. A writing group provides the crucial encouragement to keep going, to recover from rejection and submit new work.

"The group believes in me as a writer, so I am better able to believe in myself," Deborah says. "I am always impressed with the quality of our group's writing—the creativity and the willingness to share deep emotion—which inspires me to do the same."

Laurel adds, "For me, an invaluable benefit of the writing group is the affirmation it offers my work. Who else would know about this cast of made-up characters who inhabit my dreams or the twists and turns in plot that haunt my waking thoughts? Who else would share the anxiety of facing the blank page during an uninspired moment or the joy at having a scene unfold effortlessly? A writing group is like an extended family that is familiar with your inner world."

Ordinary life does not adequately prepare the writer for the task at hand. Most people do not understand the drive that compels us to write. Being with others who share the same obsession provides us with the courage to persevere. We don't seem so odd; there are others like us.

Writer Red Smith said, "There's nothing to writing. All you do is sit down at a typewriter and open a vein." Charlene adds, "This is why I belong to a writing group. If I'm going to bleed all over the page, I want the encouragement from my sister writers who will be there to stem the flow and sew up the gaping wounds."

nourishing the woman writer

Women have many demands on their time: children, parents, keeping a home, career deadlines, and time for self. How does today's woman carve out space in her hectic schedule to pursue her dream of writing? Our answer is with the support of a writing group.

The strength and encouragement of group members keep the writer going when life is pounding at the door demanding her limited resources. There are plenty of times when our writing slips into the background while the rest of life demands center stage. The support of a group helps to keep this in balance.

As Sue says, "I need to affirm that I am an artist. Sadly, life's demands can outweigh this affirmation. Artists need to be nurtured, sustained, and fed. However, in a culture that expects women to be the nurturers of men, children, and other women, the woman artist may put herself last in line and go hungry."

Artists need time to reflect, create, and leaven ideas in a warm environment where they can be kneaded and allowed to rise. Sometimes artists need suggestions about how to handle the stress of being a contemporary woman. What better place to devote time to writing and feed the writer's soul?

> "These women have faith in my writing, enough to spend hours critiquing and offering advice on ways to improve it and make me reach for new heights."—Charlene

birthing ideas and creativity

As midwives of creativity, we help each other give birth to our writing dreams. We affirm and encourage the development of our characters so they may be raised in an atmosphere of support and caring, devoting time to their proper upbringing.

An example from Laurel's experience illustrates the power of brainstorming: "I asked for input during a weekend retreat. The dynamic among several characters in my novel wasn't working. We brainstormed possible directions until multiple paths opened where before I had seen only obstacles. In a restaurant later that night, someone in the group exclaimed, 'Laurel, that family looks like it belongs in your novel!' There sat a mother and father, twin boys in matching baseball jackets, and a daughter who appeared lost in the shuffle. This real life picture captured the essence of what I was trying to express in my novel and gave me additional ideas about characterization."

Another example of brainstorming occurred when Charlene needed a new name for a character. The group tossed numerous ones around, but none seemed to fit. On Deborah's drive home, she came up with the name "Bud." She dashed off an e-mail to Charlene, and another character was christened.

Whenever one of us gets a new concept for a writing project, we use the group as a sounding board. Telling the group makes the project real and validates its worthiness. When the wheels start spinning in creative minds, it's what if, what if, what if.

raising characters

The interconnectedness that exists among us as writers extends to our characters. They become almost real to us.

Martha described an encounter that occurred as she stood in line at the grocery store watching a middle-aged woman place a birthday cake and soda on the counter. Should this scene be added to a group member's novel about a girl with anorexia? Doesn't this woman look exactly like the character's mother? Martha wanted to reach over, tap the woman on the shoulder and say, "Your daughter won't eat that junk. The carrots are in aisle one."

Deborah thinks of her writing group members as best friends who know her better than she knows herself. "They understand the main characters in my novel as well as, if not better than, I do. They tell me when I've created unlikable characters who act uncharacteristically weak, nasty, or unfocused. Sometimes they question the motivation for a character's behavior, saying, 'I can't see your character doing that,' or 'I don't feel her grief enough.'"

announcing due dates

As described in Chapter 3, our writing group establishes a schedule several months in advance. This allows us to meet the demands of children, parents, jobs, and homes, knowing that there is a deadline.

Sue describes her need for deadlines in a world where time is at a premium. "As a writer I need someone to demand to see my work. Writing is work, and the lazy artist who dwells within me would often prefer to sit back and contemplate the beauty in the world or appreciate the words someone else used to describe it; instead I need to make a commitment to write. It was only when I took formal writing classes that I wrote on a regular basis. When I tried to write independently, days turned into weeks, months, and then years. It was too easy to change my self-imposed deadlines."

Charlene says, "There are so many occasions in daily life when the idea of heading for the blank screen is the last thing I want to do. After a hard day's work, I want to put my feet up in front of a cozy fire and pretend that writing has no hold on me. Then, midway into the rationalization, it hits me. I have to submit twenty pages to the group next week! Within minutes of sitting down at the computer, grumbling and cranky, I fall under the spell of writing and love my writing sisters once again for making these demands on me."

baring it all

When we write, we expose far more of ourselves than we care to admit. Revealing ourselves first to a caring, nurturing group of comrades keeps our emotions and egos intact. It becomes easier to show a piece of writing to someone outside the group after receiving input from the inner sanctum.

> "The caring, honest, and safe nature of our group is invaluable to me as a writer."
> —Karen

The writer's life can be wracked with anxiety and fear of exposure, humiliation, and rejection. These fears are like the monsters who lived under our childhood beds. They may not be real, but we're sure they'll stop us from making it to the next writing day. There is comfort in a group of women who face the very same monsters, day in and day out, and triumph over them.

Overcoming our fear of exposure is paramount. Deborah says, "My most creative writing, which allows my 'quirky' voice to express itself, speaks more freely when I know that my writing group will be its first audience. In my braver moments, I urge my characters to do things I might have fantasized about but would never act on. My characters escape on lawn mowers from their toddlers, learn to love their bodies while in a spa, and tackle herb gardens in full army gear. Sometimes I sit at the computer, unwilling to scratch below the surface of what is safe to say. I know my writing group will tell me to go deeper, to up the ante, and I know they are right. They inspire me to plunge to deeper and darker depths, and in that nurturing environment, I can do so."

When we tackle the hardest things to say and take a risk writing an unusual piece, and especially when we submit an essay or story to an editor, we never do so alone.

seeing and believing

In a writing group, members validate each woman's voice. The respectful, honest, and empathetic manner in which they offer feedback not only helps with the technical details of craft, but also with the delicate aspects of confidence and security. One of the most inspiring benefits that evolves from a group is watching a member work on a piece, draft after draft, and eventually find reward in publication. Knowing that each member had a hand in this creation inspires everyone to continue and reach for the same goal.

> "Revealing one's inner dreams and ambitions requires a safe haven where there are no wrong turns, no mistakes, and where every false start or exploration serves a purpose."—Laurel

Sue adds, "It is only through group feedback that I am able to measure my success. When members bring their experiences to my page and interpret its meaning—a process called metacognition—I learn through their feedback that a certain passage may not make sense. I see where I have more work to do and, through their encouragement, also learn what I have done right. My belief in myself as a writer is validated."

taking vitamins

Celebrating our work brings writers back to a sharper focus, reminding them of the purpose of the group—to nurture inspiration. When we attend readings by well-known authors, we feel that we are comrades of the author, asking questions from a writer's unique perspective. We often leave so energized by them that our own words, phrases, and images surge forth, bolstered by vitamins of inspiration.

Artist dates for readings, conferences, and workshops spark inspiration and strengthen bonds among writers. They provide an invaluable way for members to live an artist's life. It's a time for us to go out into the world and proclaim publicly that we are writers. Members can attend writing conferences and workshops, set aside writing days to plan book proposals, set goals, and renew pledges to each other. These can be days to clear clutter from lives and come forth declaring that writing is still a part of life, whether there's been a hiatus from it or even scarier, if members feel burned out.

Writer retreats also offer nourishment for the writer's soul. Once a year, the SNHWWG treats itself to a weekend retreat that offers three days

without husbands, children, dogs, cats, tele-
phones, and jobs. We nurture ourselves by writing in the cheerful camaraderie of sister artists.
We bring good food and plunk ourselves down
among beautiful mountains. We stay up late, pass
a bottle of wine, and discuss favorite books and
the life of the writer. During the day, work sessions allow us to hone troublesome plots, sharpen
characters, or develop new settings. Regardless of
the type of writing activity, we feel rejuvenated
for months.

> "I have to believe in my ability to write. Writing is a complex process. We bring our ideas and experiences to the reader by creating word pictures."—Sue

finding strength in numbers

Imagine trying to read all that has been printed about the process and craft
of writing. Now picture reading all the newly published fiction and non-fiction, every biography of a writer on A&E, every writer's magazine, article,
or web site ever produced. It would be impossible.

A writing group can pool information to keep everyone up to date.
From this wealth of knowledge, members have a chance to polish their craft
and become more immersed in the writing world.

When Karen began a short story and submitted it for feedback, both
Charlene and Martha said that it reminded them of one of Stephen
King's short stories. Charlene loaned the book to Karen so she could
examine the characterization and plot structure King used. Often other
members have read a novel or story that can be used as a model for someone else in the group.

With the varied talents of members, there is always a source to tap for
technical and grammar questions. We research for each other, share books
on craft, share submission leads, and otherwise instruct and advise. As pro-
duction began on this book, Charlene discovered a panel of literary agents
discussing how to do a non-fiction book proposal on the Book TV chan-
nel. We glean information from everywhere. It's called strength in numbers!

planting seeds: tips to get you started

Well before our time, Virginia Woolf knew the importance of a woman having the means to live an artistic life. In today's fast-track society, it is imperative that a woman writer be sustained in her creative life. A writing group can nurture, affirm, and encourage one another in ways that cannot be achieved by the individual alone. It can:

- *Affirm and encourage one another*

- *Designate time for group and writing*

- *Create and value deadlines*

- *Validate the writing self*

- *Foster camaraderie*

- *Set group dates and retreats*

- *Experiment with brainstorming*

- *Share writing resources*

- *Establish a safe environment*

Six

WHAT TO DO WHEN LIFE GETS IN THE WAY

What writer hasn't dreamt once, twice, or even daily about a writer's cabin in the woods with no distractions other than birds singing and leaves floating to the ground on a bright autumn day? For some of us, every cabin or shed we pass evokes this dream. We lust after a place like the MacDowell Colony in New Hampshire or the Writer's Retreat with locations in Colorado, Mexico, and Quebec. Meals are even left silently at the door so as not to disturb the creative process. What bliss!

We dream of such a writer's paradise where our pen can't keep up with the creative (and immediately publishable) words that flow as rapidly as a spring flood from melting mountain snows. But, hey—get real! Who do you know who really has a life like this? Not any of the members of the Southern New Hampshire Women's Writing Group! We have jobs, husbands, pets, kids ranging from pre-schoolers to adult children, piles of laundry, grocery shopping, and houses that attract dirt like magnets, not to mention other interests and hobbies. In between we squeeze in time to write in a cluttered home office stacked with bills, paperwork from our paying jobs, and our kids' artwork. The office door may be closed, but the television is blaring down the hall, and the dog is scratching at the door to get in. Add to these distractions the emotional downs of the writer, and you have the three D's of writing: distractions, discouragement and (self) doubt.

But take heart. We have several strategies to help you keep writing when life gets in the way.

dealing with distractions

One of the best methods for dealing with the distractions that pull writers away from their writing is to plan writing at a time when they are lessened or non-existent. For writers who don't have sufficient motivation to establish a schedule themselves, a writing group can help. The schedule that the SNHWWG plans out months in advance requires that all the members allow for regular time to write to meet their obligations within the group.

░ SCHEDULING VERSUS STEALING TIME

Most published authors who now write full time were initially faced with finding time to write while working jobs or caring for children full time. Mothers with young children may get up before dawn—when their energy level is higher—to write before the children are up. Stealing an hour here and there may not add up to many pages; however, establishing a regular time to write is generally much more productive.

"After ecstasy, the laundry."—Zen saying

J.K. Rowling, author of the best-selling Harry Potter series, was divorced and living on public assistance in a tiny apartment with her infant daughter when she began to write. She wrote some of her first book, *Harry Potter and the Sorcerer's Stone*, at a table in a café during her daughter's naps.

Each member of the SNHWWG has found a way to schedule time to write based on the needs and demands of both family and finances. This ranges from members who write virtually full time to those who schedule regular days to write.

Deborah thought for years that writing only happened at times of extreme inspiration or emotion. This urge was unpredictable and could never be scheduled, but that changed for her a few years ago. She found that she didn't have to wait for the muse to pay a surprise visit, but only needed to sit down to write. She was able to write almost full time when she took a leave of absence from her job to live in Europe for six months. When she returned to the states, she cut her workweek by one day, giving her a day each week devoted to writing.

When Karen first started writing, she also had a full time job. She would write in the evenings and on the weekends, when she could. As she became more serious about writing, she scheduled a half-day every other week devoted to writing. As a single parent, this meant arranging for a regular babysitter. She would often go to a neighborhood café for hours at a time to write. Gradually, she cut back on her work schedule until she was only working part-time. At each step she had to arrange for childcare or make sacrifices.

Charlene feels lucky that she has school and summer vacations. That's when the bulk of her writing gets done. Now that she has an empty nest, weekends give her time that she didn't have when all three kids were home. Having a cleaning person has been the investment of a lifetime and opened up more blocks of time to write. She recommends that to anyone who can find the money. She is also known to take a day or two off from her job, putting in the same number of hours of writing as if she's going to work.

During the school year, Sue usually schedules time to write when family members have other commitments out of the home. She finds she is more creative during the summer when her time is less structured and she can relax into her writing.

Laurel transitioned from a full time corporate career to being a freelance writer over a period of several years. She schedules her day according to the type of projects she is working on, generally designating writing for the morning and editing for the afternoon. Her biggest challenge is minimizing the interruptions that come from working at home.

> "I find that a clean house provides less of a chance of rationalizing that the dirty kitchen floor needs attention more than chapter eight of my novel."—Charlene

THE RITUAL OF WRITING

Writing on demand, as opposed to only when inspiration strikes, may require a specific activity to let the brain and the creative unconscious know that the writer is ready and willing. This activity or ritual can serve as a knock on the door to the creative world. Rituals run the gamut from fixing a pot of tea, to vacuuming, to turning on music that inspires.

Many well-known writers follow specific rituals to encourage the muse to pay a visit. Toni Morrison makes a cup of coffee while it is still dark and "watches the light come." She calls this ritual her preparation to "enter a space that I can only call nonsecular." Amy Tan surrounds herself with objects that have a personal history, like old books. She "imagines the people who once turned the pages or rubbed their palms on the surface." John Updike finds it's helpful to have an impending appointment to help him concentrate and focus, explaining, "otherwise, energy spreads itself thin. . . much time can be wasted, but in the end, it must be seized."

The writing space is important as well and varies with each writer. It can range from a home office, a computer on a table in the bedroom, or even a utility shed with lights and an electrical outlet. While the availability of a window to provide either distraction or inspiration is subject to opinion, the availability of a door that can close out the world, for at least an hour or so, is a necessity. Author Annie Dillard says that "appealing workplaces are to be avoided. One wants a room with no view, so imagination can meet memory in the dark." Stephen King wrote in the laundry room when he was getting started as a writer.

Laurel generally writes in her living room using a laptop. She sips a cup of Earl Grey tea, lights a vanilla-scented candle, and sometimes listens to classical music while working. If she feels stuck, she sets the computer aside and jots down thoughts and ideas. She also carries a small notebook in her purse so if she's out doing errands and is struck by inspiration, she can record her thoughts. She always tries to determine her starting point for the next day—whether that means beginning a new scene or having an introductory sentence—so that her momentum from the previous day is continued. She's most productive when writing in the morning, so she tries to get her writing in early, before other tasks beckon.

Karen writes anywhere and everywhere. She keeps pens and notebooks with her at all times to write when she's inspired. This way she's prepared if she has unexpected time on her hands, like waiting in traffic. The demands of life and single parenting have taught her to write whenever the opportunity is presented, without formal ritual or space.

Charlene writes primarily in her home office, but also on her sailboat (where there's no escape) and at the living room desk that overlooks the woods. Even though Stephen King faces a wall and cautions against looking out windows, that doesn't work for her. She needs to see some kind of nature. She created her writing center based on the book *Simple Abundance* by Sarah Breathnach. There is a statue of a guardian angel, candles, books on writing, and a picture frame from Sue with Zora Neale Hurston's quote, "There are years that ask questions and years that answer." Charlene likes to play music from the time period she's writing about. She doesn't eat, drink, or answer the phone when she's writing. She also has a small, stuffed Tweety

Bird that she catapults in the air when she's stumped for a word. Once she starts writing, she doesn't hear anything around her—she's "in the zone."

Sue writes in her home office where she is surrounded by file drawers devoted to submission records, publishing information, and boxes labeled with the titles of manuscripts and feedback. Although she usually writes upstairs at her desk overlooking the front yard, she sometimes writes in her journal in bed before she gets up in the morning. Other times she may take a cup of coffee and sit outside in the garden or next to the pool. She has experimented with a laptop, but she finds she is more distracted. Her husband and children have always been supportive of her interest in writing and, over the years, her teens learned to respect the times she was so caught up in the story that she seemed to have temporarily left the planet.

The ideal ritual for Deborah is to take a bike ride or walk alone first thing in the morning, after her husband has taken their daughter to school. The exercise helps to eliminate the distraction of wanting to walk or ride when she is writing, but more importantly, it provides time alone with her thoughts. She carries a small notebook and pen with her and jots down ideas, especially if she has a specific writing problem in mind, and lets ideas surface so she can play with them. When she returns home, she sits down at the computer in her home office with a tea tray. Sometimes she gives in to distractions like doing laundry or making beds, but only those distractions that last a few minutes and allow a break to better concentrate on the writing when she returns. She uses the evenings after her daughter goes to bed for editing.

staving off discouragement and self-doubt

For many writers, particularly those who are not yet published or those who have a few publications but a larger stack of rejection letters, it can be difficult to keep discouragement and self-doubt at bay. When a writer questions the quality of her writing, she may feel compelled to give up her unique voice, change to a more publishable style, or give up her writing altogether. Annie Dillard says, "The feeling that the work is magnificent, and the feeling that it is abominable, are both mosquitoes to be repelled, ignored, or killed, but not indulged." Each writer must learn to develop strategies for staying focused.

For Karen the question is not how to stay motivated to write. The hard part is staying motivated to do anything other than write. It wasn't like that

"Women never have a half-hour in all their lives (excepting before or after any-body is up in the house) that they can call their own, without fear of offending or of hurting someone."
—Florence Nightingale

in the beginning, but as she began taking herself seriously as a writer, her motivation grew and developed into a force of its own. She learned to lean on the members of her writing group for much needed affirmation and encouragement.

Laurel feels that being part of a supportive and nurturing writing group is her main coping mechanism against discouragement and self-doubt. There have been times when she's felt entirely overwhelmed and disillusioned with her writing. After completing the second draft of her novel, she was so unhappy with what she'd written that she considered giving up her dream altogether. "It was just too hard," she adds. "At the time, Charlene and I were working as writing buddies. I wrote Charlene an e-mail saying I was thinking about giving up, that perhaps I wasn't meant to be a novelist. Charlene helped me to put the situation into context, suggesting I put the project aside rather than make a hasty decision." Her support at that moment of crisis helped Laurel move beyond that second draft and start her third draft several weeks later.

After Deborah receives repeated rejections for a short story or essay, discouragement and self-doubt always make an appearance. The internal voice that whispers, "Who is she trying to kid that she's a writer?" becomes louder. One of her weapons is a newspaper article that lists the number of rejections received by several major authors for works that are now considered masterpieces. For example, George Bernard Shaw received rejections for his first five novels, and Pearl Buck received fourteen rejections for *The Good Earth*. A quick look at this list reminds her that rejection is a normal part of the process. It also helps to remind her that although publication is a public acknowledgment of one's writing, it is not the primary reason she writes. She writes because she is not a fully developed person otherwise. The writing group reaffirms that the quality of her writing makes it a worthwhile endeavor.

Charlene said she was in the thick of discouragement and self-doubt when faced with rejections while trying to market her first novel. She finds it helpful to attend readings by published authors with other group members and read books they've recommended on writing. "Just show up," Stephen King says. And he's right. When she does, she remembers what it's all about. Putting one word down on paper, then another, then another.

Sue says she would have given up writing long ago if it were not for the support of the writing group. So many times she has written something that she thought was worthless, and group members have been able to mine for the hidden gems. Taking them home to cut and polish adds enjoyment to her writing process.

helping loved ones understand

Often authors find that the non-writers in their lives do not understand the time and effort that goes into writing, particularly a novel, and may often ask if you're finished yet and what's taking so long. When some group members told family and friends they'd finished the first draft of a novel, their response was, "When is it going to get published?" They didn't understand that there may be two or three more drafts needed, followed by the difficulty of finding an agent to represent your novel.

The fact that writing is such a solitary activity, and that loved ones may feel isolated and even rejected during the writing process, may add to this. Leaving for writing group meetings may involve getting by family members who barricade the doorway asking, "You're meeting with your writing group again?"

Others may be too close to what you are writing and impose censors on your work. For writers who cut back on their full time jobs to have more time to write, family members and friends may find this behavior irresponsible or unrealistic. Since you may not be getting paid to write, they may expect you to run errands for them or babysit during your scheduled writing time.

> "[A writer] should also live with someone who can cook and who will both be with one and leave one alone."
> —Lorrie Moore

Working for hours on something that isn't as tangible to family members as weeding a flower garden or painting the bathroom can make it difficult for them to see the results of your effort.

help is on the way

There are many ways to help family and loved ones understand the need to write. Discussing the plans and projects of the writing group with family members may help them realize your commitment. Sharing your work, particularly the results of several drafts, may help them to understand the effort it takes as well as providing a tangible result of your work. You may want to share your dream of writing and being published and discuss how long you have wanted to be a writer, so they can understand its importance to you. Who knows, maybe you will inspire them to become writers or to act on their own dreams.

Writer Brenda Ueland says, "If you would shut your door against the children for an hour a day and say: 'Mother is working on her five-act tragedy in blank verse!' you would be surprised how they would respect you. They would probably all become playwrights."

Some family members understand, even at a young age. When J.K. Rowling's daughter was asked what mommies do, she replied, "Mommies write."

In Sue's family, creativity was encouraged in her children as they were growing up. "Years of carefully stepping around Lego villages sprawled across the floor and finding crayons stuck in every nook and cranny imaginable resulted in children who understand and respect the creative process. My son built block villages that stayed set up for weeks at a time, and would carefully revise them to suit the needs of the little imaginary people who lived there. My daughter never traveled anywhere without crayons and paper and her artwork showed up on the refrigerators in many of the homes we visited." Her children are adults now and brag that their mother is a writer.

Charlene's family has also benefited from her writing. She serves as a built-in editor for school papers. They also see her as a role model to never stop striving toward their dreams. They are very proud of her writing penchant. She feels blessed that she doesn't have to break through barricades, only the dog, to go to group meetings. If anything, she has to spy on her husband to prevent the pilfering of her writing to share with friends, colleagues, and family members!

Karen's young son sometimes complains when she is off to yet another writing group meeting, but she has set up a routine that's special for him as well. He has "date night" with his favorite babysitter, and they go out to dinner. Karen tells her son frequently that she is a writer, and she lets him see that writing and the group are important to her. Karen finds that frequently talking about her writing plans and projects has helped her family members take her writing seriously and understand its importance.

Deborah has frequently discussed her lifelong dream of being a writer with her husband. She feels fortunate that her husband is extremely supportive of her need to write and is her first reader for most of her work. It is more difficult for her young daughter to understand the need for privacy when Mommy shuts the office door to write. Her daughter is often not happy when Deborah leaves for writing group, but her husband's support helps to smooth things over, even when it requires that he leave work early.

When Laurel left her corporate career, some of her relatives and work acquaintances thought she was crazy. Fortunately, her husband was very understanding; particularly considering the loss of income meant they'd have to be more careful financially. Then there's the fact that he is featured in much of her writing!

Other writing group members can provide the understanding of the need to write, as well as the support, when it is absent from family and friends.

you can do it!

Unless you live alone with no interruptions at all (and who doesn't at least have to do the laundry at times?), distractions are a part of life. Every writer can find a way to schedule time to write, while balancing the demands of her own life. If the writer's life is calling, you will find a way to make it a reality. A writing group can help you say good-bye to the three D's of distractions, discouragement, and (self) doubt.

Seven

REALIZING THE WRITER'S DREAM

Whether the goal is to finish a quilt, read and discuss a book, walk five miles every morning, or help each other improve writing skills, the primary focus of any group is to provide encouragement and support for members' goals and dreams. Through this support, individual members discover internal resources of strength. The dynamics of the Southern New Hampshire Women's Writing Group sheds light like a prism, casting colorful rays onto its members and their work. The group's support, skill level, knowledge base, and nurturance fuel each member.

group differences add light, texture, and dimension

Although our commonalities combine to create a group personality that everyone is comfortable with, the diversity of our personal interests, careers, and personalities adds a spice to the stew. Members benefit from rich feedback and expertise because our membership includes a range of backgrounds, careers, hobbies, and ages.

Various backgrounds can provide a writing group with areas of specialty, and everyone benefits. In the SNHWWG, Laurel has a gift for trimming verbose language while catching redundancy of words. She is also one of the group's experts on punctuation. This, coupled with Sue's mastery of sentence structure and grammar, more than covers us in the editorial department.

Charlene and Barbara are tuned to the power of metaphor and creating strong, female characters. Karen is our specialist in the mystery genre, using her knowledge of plot to help us "up the ante."

Deborah brings travel information, facts about European culture, and idiosyncratic details for characters. Along with Karen, who writes travel books, and Martha, who also travels, our settings are enhanced with rich and authentic data that help bring our novels to life.

> "In developing our child characters with the help of the group, we benefit from the education and experience of mothers who have raised them, teachers who have taught them, and counselors who have supported them."
> —Charlene

Martha is our resident queen of details, noting inconsistencies in passage of time, characters' hair color (brown in one chapter and red in another—oops!), and other details that don't add up.

Food and gardening enthusiasts transform those aspects of our writing with their experiences and information, counselors express psychological concerns in character development, editors and technical writers gently chide for too many "that's" and not enough commas, and explain the difference between em dashes and hyphens.

Familiarity with different genres of writing helps us give good feedback on plot and structure. Suggestions are often made to read books and authors who have mastered an element of writing that one of us may be struggling with. When Charlene was challenged by point of view issues in her novel, which includes five main characters, group members were ready with titles such as *The Poisonwood Bible, The Robber Bride*, and *The Saving Graces*—all examples of novels written in multiple points of view. Also, many members read books on the writing process by famous authors as well as books on craft. Since we can't all physically read every one of these books, we share information from them and recommend only the best.

Our ages are diverse enough for members to benefit from the experiences and memories of baby boomers as well as those of the "thirtysomethings." Group membership spans from the thirties to fifties—and who knows—perhaps we will find a twentysomething or an eightysomething in our midst in the future. Diversity of age is looked upon as a fringe benefit that complements our group dynamic.

We are not presently an ethnically diverse group—another dynamic to look forward to—so we rely upon books by ethnic writers as well as depend on present members' experiences, ethnic backgrounds such as Barbara's Greek heritage, education through travel, and multicultural perspectives in general.

We all enjoy writing nonfiction as well as fiction. Personal essays, poetry, professional articles for journals, even song lyrics, find their way into the feedback lineup, giving us practice critiquing all kinds of writing. At times, we may express concern over perceived limitations in critiquing some of these forms, thinking we don't have the expertise required to give accurate, helpful feedback to our poets and essayists. However, the poets learn about structure from the essayists, the essayists learn about imagery and metaphor from the poets. Meanwhile, Barbara, our songwriter, teaches all of us about the sound of words and how they resonate within us. We learn so much from each other's writing!

Our fiction writing stretches from women's fiction to romance writing to mystery and intrigue, and back around to young adult writing. We blush at the wild sex scenes in a romantic novel and wonder where they are in another, worry about adolescent protagonists in a coming of age story, and guess at killers in a mystery. Sometimes, we move along so smoothly in our reading of another member's pages that we forget to critique as we go!

Our diverse elements create a rainbow of talent, skill, and knowledge that are prized by each of us; each member is illuminated by a different color from the prism, refracting light as she moves forward toward that once elusive dream that is now within her grasp.

how group dynamics transform the individual writer's craft

When writing in solitude, even the most polished writer can question if her characters are three dimensional, her plot sustains itself throughout the novel, or whether there is sufficient dialogue.

In a writing group, we are given feedback every step of the way, from first to final draft. Each member brings the talents and skills of seasoned readers who are familiar with the various elements of craft such as character development, point of view, plot, dialogue, details, voice, and setting. Another important advantage is that members are also familiar enough with each other's writing to recognize when a piece is shaping up to publication standards. One of the most exciting comments we hear from one another is "Send it in!"

CHARACTER DEVELOPMENT

Character development is significantly influenced by the dynamics of a group. Author Janet Burroway says, "As a writer, you may have the lucky, facile sort of imagination to which characters spring full-blown, complete with gestures, histories, and passions. Or it may be that you need to explore in order to exploit, to draw your characters out gradually and coax them into being." Group members can coax hidden personality traits, cajole emotional layers, and help create backstory for each other's characters. The depth of feedback alone can make otherwise one-dimensional characters into three dimensional, colorful, and often quirky people running around in our novels.

In Sue's young adult novel, *No Goodbyes*, the character of the protagonist's mother seemed distant and unclear. Sue felt that the questions the group asked forced her to define her character's personality and motivation much more than she originally thought was sufficient. Deborah notices that she sometimes gets caught up in the plot of her novel, *Searching for Vincent*, making her protagonist, Kat, behave in ways that aren't always consistent with her character. "Kat's actions may work well for the plot, but the group always catches it if it's not consistent with her personality." A character in Martha's novel went from being a woman to a man, becoming Conrad instead of Connie, because the group felt that a man would make a more interesting character and add tension to the plot.

> "I feel at times that I'm making up these little people and I've lost my mind."
> —Carolyn Chute

Getting to know each other's characters creates a stronger bond within the group as we all remain attentive to each other's characters' needs as if they are family.

POINT OF VIEW

Finding the right point of view for a story can be a challenge. In the SNHWWG we witness each other begin novels and short stories in one point of view and then attempt a second draft and sometimes a third in yet another—a rather heroic undertaking.

Laurel's novel, *Waking Up the Fenders*, is the best illustration of this. "I struggled with the point of view of my novel, scrapping the first two drafts because the story wasn't coming out the way I intended. I switched to the first person in my third draft and the group immediately gave me the feedback that I had found my voice. The story became more accessible and the characters more authentic than in other drafts."

Charlene's change of point of view in a short story from first to third person helped the piece be accepted for publication. The switch to third person provided a distance from the subject that was needed in order to move the story forward. Trying the different point of view was a suggestion from a group member.

We are strengthened by how improved subsequent drafts are when the writer discovers that her voice is enriched and made more authentic. We are encouraged by each other to try out new techniques because we know we can do so within the safety of the group.

PLOT

Plot is an element of craft that we all struggle with at times. Elizabeth Berg says, "There are two kinds of writers, those who start with a plot and those who end up with one." Some writers outline their work to address this while others feel more comfortable writing through the first draft and then working on plot in the second draft. No matter what the process, the group profoundly affects the final outcome.

As we struggle with plot points and read voraciously on the subject, we depend on each other for help to overcome sagging, nagging, boring, or nonexistent plots. Some of our best discussions on this element of craft have taken place at our weekend retreats when we have the time to talk about each other's novels and brainstorm more effective ways to improve the plotline.

During one of these brainstorms, we pleaded with Deborah to allow her protagonist, Kat, to have an affair with another character. What better way to spice it up? The vote is still out on that one, but often in these group discussions, we come up with ideas and twists that will help the writer improve her story. Karen's novel has also fallen victim to this group desire for two of her characters in her mystery novel to be attracted to each other. More tension, we say, more romance. Karen shakes her head, saying "No, that's for the sequel!" Okay, so sometimes we cross the line, but each member's ability to sort out the feedback is strong and functioning.

Sue's young adult novel has a middle school protagonist abducted by her mother. Comments from members who have been through divorce and custody issues shed emotional light that helped shape the plot. Sue added strong characters that moved in and changed events. The plot took on a life of its own and the climax and resolution changed dramatically.

Stephen King says, "When you write a book, you spend day after day scanning and identifying the trees. When you're done, you have to step back and look at the forest."

DIALOGUE

Dialogue should move the plot forward, add conflict, and most of all, enhance character development. Writer Anne Lamott says, "Dialogue is the way to nail character, so you have to work on getting the voice right. . . If you can get their speech mannerisms right, you will know what they're wearing and driving and maybe thinking, and how they were raised, and what they feel."

The no-nonsense, crisp dialogue in Karen's mystery novel, *Cleaning the Slate*, offers a model for the rest of us. The mystery genre is an ideal place to learn the importance of spare dialogue when that is what's needed. Group members have all benefited from reading the book, *Self-Editing for Fiction Writers*, with its chapters on dialogue, and we all provide better feedback as a result. We are always on the lookout to break up large amounts of narrative, knowing that the balance between dialogue and narrative is critical, asking each other where there should be scenes with dialogue and where it could be cut. Seasoned readers have a gift for recognizing what's enough and what's not.

> "Dialogue is not real speech—it's the illusion of real speech."
> —Ernest Hemingway

In the SNHWWG members are all careful to keep our characters' conversations honest. Karen's mystery novel has a character who must remind us in dialogue that he is Texan. Sue's young adult novel has a cast of ethnic characters who express subtleties in their speech. Charlene's novel, *Dream Street*, has a troupe of "almost" juvenile delinquents who use profanity and street language. The nuances are staggering, and a group full of dialogue vigilantes is a good thing to have around!

DETAILS

Details provide a richness and authenticity to one's writing. Some writers have a natural tendency to load their first drafts with details. Other writers barely include any, just getting down the story. A writing group can help the writer find a perfect balance.

"Ideas come from the strangest places."
—Joyce Carol Oates

What constitutes too many details and what happens when there are too few? Deborah's novel is a great example of this struggle. She explains, "Since my initial interest in writing this novel was to relive the time I lived in the Netherlands, I'm only too happy to include every little detail, much of which is irrelevant to the plot. The group points this out in a kind way, and I know they are right." The end result of the group's input is to make the novel stronger by cutting details that would otherwise bog down the story.

Karen states that her first draft writing is often skeletal and that she needs to go back to fill in the blanks. She often looks to the group for ideas on where more information is needed.

Group members point out locations in the plot that could use more details—characters that need more colorful wardrobes, scenes that describe the weather, time, and season, and dinners that include what the characters are eating. What shows were on TV in the time period of the novel? What movies were showing? Who was the president? What music was popular? What one member misses in the way of detail, another points out, all the while paying attention to that perfect balance one recognizes in a good piece of writing.

VOICE

Author Josip Novakovich says, "Novice writers go around looking for their voices just as people used to go around looking for themselves." Some writers may find their natural voice early while others may have to work harder to discover it. Sometimes group members can recognize when a member has "hit her stride," or found her voice, before the writer herself.

The group nurtures this invisible element and pounces when it peeks out at us from a

"You know it when you see it in another writer's work, yet don't always see it in your own. Particularly when I've written something quirky, the group often comments on the unique voice, and I think—Eureka!— I've found that elusive quality called voice."
—Deborah

member's writing. "There it is! You've nailed it!" These are common shouts when we announce the birth of a member's voice. It's similar to coming home to Boston's Cheers bar and being recognized and patted on the back. Everyone's happy to see you. Everyone knows your voice.

SETTING

Setting is yet another way of helping our stories be fully realized. The rooms we construct around our characters tell the reader more about them, add to the tension of the plot, and help the reader visualize the story. Anne Lamott uses the term "set design" to illustrate setting. As the group watches the construction of each member's "sets," all of the elements of diversity meld together and create worlds, countries, states, cities, neighborhoods, living rooms, or gardens that are rich in detail. In essence, we help each other design our sets.

In our novels, we travel the country from Nashville to Texas to the slums of Washington, D.C.; we visit a farm in Olney, Illinois; we walk the tough streets of Boston; we visit a swimming hole in the White Mountains of New Hampshire, and the art world in the Netherlands. We help each other add color, lighting, and props to our sets. Then we people them with our characters and watch them thrive.

sharing our writing process

How can a writing group help the writer define her process—her individual way of transforming thought into print? Each writer ultimately faces the blank page alone, but group members can learn from each other by listening to what works for one and what doesn't work for another.

In the SNHWWG we have assisted each other in defining the process that helps us put words on paper. Laurel says, "A benefit to being in a writing group is that I can observe the writing process of my fellow group members to enhance my own. I'm the type of writer who struggles with every word, striving to make each draft as polished as possible. Other group members quickly work through their first draft, focusing on getting the story on paper. When I feel stuck in my own writing, I remind myself that it's okay—and sometimes desirable—to move quickly." All members feel that by observing each other's process, they can sometimes overcome blocks and avoid getting bogged down in detail.

Stephen King rarely plots his novel before writing. He says, "I distrust plot for two reasons: first, because our lives are largely plotless, even when you add in all our reasonable precautions and careful planning; and second, because I believe plotting and the spontaneity of real creation aren't compatible."

Deborah leans more toward this philosophy as she says, "I'm the type of writer who just jumps in with both feet. I start with a situation, a character, or a setting and often have little to no idea what will happen next. By hearing about the many other structured approaches that other members use, I am able to expand my repertoire, especially when I feel stuck."

On the other end of the spectrum is author John Irving who says, "I not only write a very plot-oriented novel, I write outlines. I know before I write the first sentence where the end of the book is, and what all the important details of the book are. . . . I spend a year or 18 months making a street map of a novel before I ever begin to write."

Charlene finds this style compatible with her own. She draws the plot line, showing plot points and other key scenes, then fills in the blanks during the writing process. "Even a sketchy map is helpful to get me through that first petrified forest," she says.

Writer Grace Paley says, "I might write four lines or I might write twenty. I subtract and I add until I really hit something. You don't always whittle down, sometimes you whittle up."

Recognizing that each writer has her own process is important. Sue feels that being exposed to techniques other writers use expands her own writing process. Group members watch each other experiment with innovative ways to advance their writing and are encouraged to try these new techniques.

In the SNHWWG we have developed many strategies that help us with our writing process. Use of character sketches to flesh out personalities has deepened character development. Finding pictures of people we imagine as characters in our novels helps those who need visual enhancement. Taking field trips to settings to "see" details adds texture, smell, and color. Sketching out physical settings to better define our characters' worlds is another visual technique. Using clustering to brainstorm ideas has worked for some. As a group, we have used our creativity to devise ways to enhance our process. Group exercises can be found in Chapter 10.

the dream realized

Each writer begins her writing career with an inward vision to find her voice. Nancy Slonim Aronie says, "We carry [our stories] around in our bodies, our cells, our souls, for our whole lives." At some point, each writer makes a decision to seek a process that will help her translate these stories into words on paper. She begins to call herself a writer and to take very seriously this drive to be heard through words.

Sue says, "I decided to be a writer when I was ten. When I told my father, he laughed and explained that writers don't make enough money to live on. The dream evaporated into thin air. Twenty-five years later, I took a writing class. Twelve years after that, I have been published and we have this book contract."

Karen is realizing her writer's dream in Technicolor! She is writing a column on single parenting issues for a local paper as well as writing travel guides. She has often verbalized her wish to become a full-time writer and leave the high-tech world behind. The validation that came from the group helped her believe in herself as a writer.

> "Have the courage to write whatever your dream is for yourself."
> —May Sarton

A writing group has helped us all make writing a major part of our creative lives. As we draw from each other's lives and experiences, we learn the craft and witness each other's learning process along the way. We teach each other, and we identify our strengths and weaknesses. We help one another find the real meanings and themes in our work. Perhaps most telling of the group's success to help each member realize her dream is that all are now published authors!

Eight

INTRODUCING YOUR WRITING TO THE PUBLISHING WORLD

You pick up a pen and let your thoughts spill onto the page. Then what? Do you have plans for your creation other than using the pages to line the cat's litter box because you don't want anyone to see them?

Authors compose for different reasons: for the sheer enjoyment of the creative process, as a form of comfort or personal therapy, or merely to share information. Some write as a way to record their lives or cope with situations. Author Dorothy Allison explains, "I'm the only one who can tell the story of my life and say what it means."

Each writer needs to decide what she wants to do with her work. The idea of publication takes a certain mindset, like wearing a new outfit for the first time—you know you will get some reactions to it, but you're not sure what they will be. If the first person who sees you says something negative, you may be tempted to go home and change your clothes. Sharing your writing requires the courage to let yourself become vulnerable—it's like submitting for feedback on a large scale. If you read it to the cat and she flips her tail at you and stalks out of the room, you

> "All those writers who write about their childhood! Gentle God, if I wrote about mine you wouldn't sit in the same room as me."
> —Dorothy Parker

may wonder if the thoughts you have written on the page are worthy of human attention. A reaction like that could tempt you to go back to the litter box idea. That's when you need your writing group!

the publishing dream

When the members of the Southern New Hampshire Women's Writing Group first began to meet, publication was a far off planet where writers like Maya Angelou, Elizabeth Berg, and Anita Shreve resided—a place where caged birds fly free, mothers don't die, and husbands are faithful. A few of the members already knew they wanted to be published authors but were uncertain about how to make that happen. Karen dreamed of doing travel writing full time. Laurel and Barbara, who both had articles published previously, joined the group with the dream of writing a novel.

As group members received feedback each month, we came to understand that there are different ways to share our work. We used our computers to print pages so that group members could read them during the week before our meeting. We published orally by reading our work to each other. As we continued to revise and share, phrases like "That's really good," "I'd like a copy to share with a friend," and "You should submit that," began to slip into conversations. Our confidence began to grow. This gave us the courage to seek a wider audience by submitting our work outside of our group.

What is your writing dream? Are you ready to jump in the water and swim for it? Or are you just getting your toes wet? Whatever your state of mind may be on the subject, if you know you're a writer, read on!

the path to publishing

If being published is one of your goals, consider your options. Each time you read your piece aloud, write a letter to a friend or the newspaper, submit for feedback, or write anything that others will read, you have just published your work. If you read your work on public radio or post something on a web site, you have expanded your audience.

Self publishing is an option on a larger scale. Rick Steves, author of *Europe Through the Back Door*, duplicated and stapled his first editions to sell to local travelers. His work was finally picked up by a publisher after he had made several revisions. Another example of self publishing is Frank Capra's movie, *It's a Wonderful Life*, which started out as a holiday story that Philip Van Doren Stern wrote and shared with family members.

Laura Doyle's path to publication also started with self publishing, then took a series of unexpected turns. *The Surrendered Wife* is the story of strategies Laura tried in an effort to regain a closer relationship with her husband. Laura and her husband decided to share their story with other women who were interested in improving their marriages, so the couple contracted and paid someone to publish 2,000 copies. These sold out after a month. Spurred on by this success, Laura's husband submitted their book to ten agents, drawing attention from an agent who brought the book to Simon & Schuster. The *Los Angeles Times* published an article about the discussion groups Laura led for women to talk about their marriages. The title of the book, combined with testimonies from so many women, created controversy which drew national attention. End of story? This self published book, with its small, local beginning, ended up on the *New York Times* best-selling book list.

Inspired by a volume of prose that was self published by a local writing group, the members of the SNHWWG decided to embark on the same journey. After selecting and revising pieces of their work, each member sent her newly polished piece to Laurel, who used her experience as a former technical writer and editor to format a booklet called *A Journey Of Words*. This gave us a tremendous sense of accomplishment.

It would be nice if the road from word processor to publication was straightforward and clearly marked. But, as the Doyles found out, each author has his or her own tale to tell about a process that can have many twists and turns, as well as stops and starts. The road to publication is similar to embarking on a trip. Talking to others who have been there before helps you gain an understanding of the layout of the destination, important words to know, and events that may occur while you are there. This information can enhance the entire trip and result in savings of time and money. This is also true for those who desire to make the journey from unpublished to published writer; understanding the language, events, and markers along the way can help make the journey a smoother one.

> "A professional writer is an amateur who didn't quit."
> —Richard Bach

Often, the more writing experience an author has, the more likely her work will be published. This record of a writer's experience is known as publishing credits and may be developed by having work published without receiving monetary compensation. Letters to the editor, local news stories, recognition in local writing contests, and writing for newsletters may be included as publishing credits. Small magazines and professional and literary journals often pay for work by sending authors a number of free copies of the publication. All of this experience helps to establish the credibility of the author.

It was helpful when Laurel shared her list of publishing credits, which is included in Part Three, with other group members to use as an example. If you know an author, or attend a public reading or workshop given by one, ask if she or he will share a copy of her or his publishing credits. Some will even have brochures or websites with details about their publishing history.

defining the destination

Once a piece has been completed, critiqued by the writing group, and revised, an author may decide it is time to send it out. When that time comes, she will need a strategy.

Publishing houses come in all sizes, and when an author decides to submit a piece of work, she needs to research what size press would best suit her work. Large publishing houses are more competitive and less personal because they work with hundreds of authors. They sometimes give advance payment to those with proven track records. Small presses often work more closely with authors but probably publish a limited number of books each year. Some authors begin by sending their work to large publishing houses and work their way down a list. Others may feel intimidated by the larger houses and begin by submitting to smaller houses.

An author interested in submitting short stories, essays, or poems to magazines or newspapers should study several copies of each to decide which best matches her work in philosophy and genre. She will also need to have realistic expectations regarding the size of the magazine publisher; it is usually easier to be published by a smaller press than a well known magazine. Authors who submit to magazines often keep a list of potential markets and make changes to the piece to tailor it to fit the needs of different publications. If the author has retained her rights to the piece, it can be remarketed and sold more than once.

An author also needs to decide if she will send simultaneous submissions—submitting the same piece to multiple places at one time. If she decides to submit to multiple places in one mailing, she is eliminating the possibility of being published by houses that do not take simultaneous submissions. If she decides to wait, she is losing valuable time. How does a writer know the right path to take?

Each year Writer's Digest Books publishes a catalogue of potential markets called *Writer's Market.* This volume lists hundreds of potential publishers for all types of writing. It includes information such as what each editor is looking for, how many books they publish each year, whether they accept simultaneous submissions, how many queries they receive, the number of publications from unagented authors, a time line for an expected response, where the publishing house is located, and who to contact. The information is arranged by genre, as well as alphabetically, and is also available on CD ROM. This book is a gold mine of information for an author looking for a good match for her manuscript.

One strategy for using the book is to make a list of terms describing you and your piece of writing using the same terms as those used in *Writer's Market*. Then highlight those same categories in the descriptions given in *Writer's Market*. For example, if you are a first time author seeking to market a mystery novel, you might highlight the word mystery in the fiction area listed under each publisher, the percentage of books they publish from first time authors, and if they accept unagented work. The entries where you have done the most highlighting may prove to be good matches for your piece. If you want to avoid marking up your book, do this comparative analysis on your computer.

It is also a good idea to use your computer to keep a record of submissions. Use a database program and create fields to list where and when you submitted, the contact person, and their response. This information will help you know when it is time to follow up on your piece and will come in handy the next time you are ready to submit for publication.

You can also use your writing group to get ideas about publishing. Members are familiar with what you are working on, and when they see calls for submissions, they will pass the information along, knowing that your work may be exactly what the publisher is looking for. Many SNHWWG meetings have begun with a flurry of papers being distributed around the table—all calls for submissions which members have found!

manuscript meets world

Marketing a piece of writing is much like planning a trip. If an author decides to hire a literary agent, her or his job is much like that of a travel agent. Both of these positions involve sales based planning and leg work. On the other hand, if the author decides to send her work directly to publishers, she needs to understand how to dispatch it safely to the intended destination. Authors usually send magazine submissions with only a query letter. However, some book publishers will only accept submissions from literary agents. Knowing what to submit to whom requires research, but the one thing that all publishers and agents have in common is an expectation for high quality work, free of grammatical and typographical errors.

Laurel shares her experience from when she published a newsletter for women called *The Aurora.* "My work partner and I received a variety of submissions from essays to poetry. While most were professionally presented, some were laden with typographical errors and silly mistakes. The latter went immediately into a slush pile . . . never to see the light of day. It was a shame because the submissions might have had merit but, as both publishers and editors, we were too busy to examine them. We felt if those authors hadn't taken the time to submit works of high caliber when others had, why should we invest the time to review them?"

> "Each of us has changed from individual, mostly unpublished writers— full of ideas—to published writers who change through the magic of the group process."—Sue

Publishers usually have a preconceived idea of what type of writing they plan to publish and require certain components in marketing packages. These components will differ depending on whether the work is fiction or nonfiction. Fiction publishers expect the work to be complete and include a query letter, several chapters of the book or novel, a synopsis or chapter outline, an author biography, writing samples, and/or a list of publishing credits. Publishers of non-fiction work will expect a proposal that includes a query letter, sample chapter(s), a chapter outline, and a comparative analysis of similar pieces. Non-fiction work is not usually expected to be complete at the time the proposal is made. Different agents or agencies may request any combination of these components.

When the members of the SNHWWG decided to write a proposal for this book, we spent almost as much time researching what each of the components included as we did writing the proposal. It was very helpful when local author and former writing group member, Susanne Whayne, shared one of her marketing packages with us.

What's the scoop on the components of a marketing package? Entire books have been written on the subject, but here's a thumbnail sized version.

One key to open the door for publication is the *query letter*. This is where an author sells the idea for a piece of work, while at the same time demonstrating her writing ability. Editor Tara Horton advises writers to think of a query letter as a job interview. A good query letter sells a manuscript by catching the editor's attention and summarizing the contents of the submission. It is focused and creative and is usually one page in length. Once a writer has an understanding of these basic principles, the writing group is a good place to test it out. The reactions of the group members will indicate how the agent, editor, or publisher may respond, and their suggestions can lead to improvements.

Charlene relates how the writing group helped her with this process. "I definitely dragged my feet when it came time to send queries to agents on my novel, *Dream Street*. As I look back on it now, it was pure, unadulterated fear that blocked my ability to take the next step into the publishing world. Until then, I don't think I had really thought about the exposure that was involved. Only group members had seen the manuscript. With their encouragement, I set some goals and used feedback slots to submit query letters and synopses. This pushed me along, and finally I had a package ready to send to agents. Once again, it was the group that facilitated this."

Sue also benefited from the group's assistance. "In the first draft of my query letter, I referred to the number of children who are abducted in the United States each year. When this statistic, and the reason for including it, were not clear to the members of the writing group, I knew I had more work to do. I had also pointed out my lack of publication credits and the group recommended that I replace that information with other accomplishments."

A *synopsis* provides a summary of a novel while focusing on important plot points and descriptions of characters. A *non-fiction book proposal* will include an annotated chapter outline. An *author biography* is written in the third person, present tense, and may include a recent photo. *Publishing credits* look much like a combination of a resume and a bibliography, listing what the author has written from the most recent to the oldest. A *comparative analysis* is a brief description of published work similar to the piece being submitted. It is helpful to point out differences here, especially if the submission is strong where the previously published pieces are not. Publishers and agents may want any combination of the above.

When the members of the group went on our second spring retreat, many of us were ready to begin the publication process. Each member brought resources about the subject to share with the group. Throughout the weekend, we made trial runs at creating different parts of a marketing package and shared our work with others to get ideas for improvement. One fun exercise was writing book jacket descriptions about each other's novels. These activities allowed us to get feedback about each submission component from our sister writer. We have continued to work on our marketing packages, and we keep the components on file to send out when agents and publishers request additional information.

advice about agents

Literary agents represent an author's work for a percentage-based fee. Many are former editors whose knowledge and expertise can help authors maneuver their way through the literary world. They often know what publishers and editors are looking for, and their experience and professional contacts can expedite a contract offer.

If a writer decides she would like to be represented by an agent, she will need to mail a query letter and marketing package much the same way she would if she was submitting her work to a publisher. And, much like publishers, literary agencies also come in a variety of sizes—from large New York City firms to individual agents who work out of home offices. Writer's Digest Books offers a volume similar to *Writer's Market* called the *Guide to Literary Agents* that gives an overview of literary agents and agencies. Additional resources include *The Insider's Guide to Getting an Agent* as well as books and web sites listed in Part Three.

The members of our group learned an important lesson about agents through the experience of one of our members. Charlene's novel was being considered by two agencies. After several weeks had passed, one of the agencies withdrew its interest, so she signed with the second one. Although the second agency was listed as non-fee charging, it required a payment to cover the cost of copying and mailing her manuscript to publishing houses. Charlene reflects on her experience with new insight. "My novel was tied up for almost a year after submitting to an agency that looked legitimate, but had misrepresented themselves."

hot-off-the-press tips for selecting an agent

1. Never pay an agent to read or represent your work unless she or he has obtained a publishing contract for you. Even then, payment should be made according to the terms previously agreed upon in the contract.

2. Try to find an agent who is a member of the Association of Author's Representatives (AAR) that requires its members to agree to meet professional standards. Members are listed at the AAR web site: www.publishersweekly.com/aar.

3. Be wary of form letter acceptances. Agents who are truly interested in representing you will usually contact you personally, either by phone or e-mail.

4. Check out the prospective agent on the Internet at www.literaryagents.org.

5. Review all contracts with a lawyer or someone who is knowledgeable about literary contracts.

6. Be aware of exceptionally good payments—this may mean you are giving up some of the literary rights you may like to retain.

7. When you sign the contract, pop a bottle of champagne!

putting it in perspective

If you feel overwhelmed at the prospect of submitting your work for publication, you're in good company. Author Mary Higgins Clark was rejected 40 times before selling her first story. Alex Haley received 200 rejections before *Roots* was published. Dr. Seuss' first book was rejected by 24 publishers. After years of work by many people, the *Chicken Soup for the Soul* series was initially rejected by 140 publishers. Three years later it made the best seller lists of the *New York Times*, the *Washington Post*, *Publishers Weekly*, and *USA Today*.

Sometimes editors will write handwritten messages on returned manuscripts. This attention is very encouraging and can help an author to cope with rejection. Betsy Lerner, author of *The Forest for the Trees*, compares the type of notes an author receives to the rungs on a ladder. The bottom rung is the generic form letter. This is followed by the form letter with a few encouraging words written on it. The next rung is a personal note to the author. One step above that is the letter that rejects the work submitted but invites the author to send more work. Of course, the letter that accepts the writer's work is the top step!

A little humor can also help take the sting out of rejection. In spite of careful research about where to submit the proposal for this book, the authors of *A Group of One's Own* received the following letter:

Dear group,

   Thank you for your book submission. Unfortunately our listing is inaccurate. We specialize in books on subjects concerning classic fishing tackle and the makers of fishing tackle, and select subjects on western history. Since your manuscript does not fit into our area of interest, we would not be interested, but good luck with your endeavors.

This news was, of course, followed by e-mails between group members full of jokes about fishing and puns about hooking an interested editor.

Having a piece "out there" makes getting the mail an exciting part of the day. Deborah says she tries to weigh the envelope in her hands to guess if it's an acceptance or a rejection, while Laurel describes walking around the house for an hour before finding the courage to open it. On one occasion Karen was really excited to find a large package from a publisher, only to learn that the publisher had returned her entire manuscript. When Charlene was contacted by a well known agency, they called her home and spoke with her husband. Little did he know that after speaking with him, they called her at her work place, taking the wind out of his congratulatory announcement when she arrived home.

> "Your success as a writer will probably not depend on how well you write so much as in how you handle rejections."
> —Gilbert Morris, Ph.D.

If you believe you have a message in your writing that others will enjoy, hang in there! Remind yourself that rejection letters are not personal, nor are they an evaluation of the quality of your manuscript. Many submissions will not be read because the publisher or agent was able to determine from your query that the piece was not what they were looking for.

Laurel shared that the group helps her to deal with rejection by reminding her that it is a natural part of the publication process. She says that the group acts as a sounding board, letting her know if they think the piece needs more work, if it would be better suited for another publication, or if she should just keep trying. This feedback helps her to view rejection as a learning experience rather than reason to give up hope for getting the piece published.

Take refuge in the encouragement and wisdom of your sister writing group members. Be proactive about handling the emotions that come with rejection letters. Share stories about authors who struggled before making it in the publishing world. Reread the positive feedback group members gave you on the rejected piece or perhaps the one on which you are currently working. It may help to redirect that negative energy by beginning a new creative endeavor. You could follow F. Scott Fitzgerald's example and paper the wall in your writing space with your rejection letters. But whatever you decide to do, remember—perseverance is the fuel needed for this journey!

Nine

Time to celebrate

It's time to pop open the bubbly and let the corks fly! Celebration is a form of acknowledgment. When we celebrate another's success, we acknowledge that person's hard work and perseverance. As writers, we're often so focused on completing a work and moving on that we forget to pause to celebrate our journey. That's where the spirit of celebration comes in—to help us reflect on where we've been and to remind us of where we're going. So let the festivities begin!

you go, sister writer!

When you are part of a writing group, you are surrounded by individuals who understand what it means to be a writer. In the company of women writers, you are with kindred spirits who share your desire to compose meaningful words while juggling multiple tasks and responsibilities. In a writing group everyone sees how much effort is involved to bring a work to fruition. There may be unexpected sidetrips, moments of feeling lost, and unwelcome twists and turns—not to mention those pesky rejection letters. Taking the time to acknowledge the successes and accomplishments of each member—as well as the collective accomplishments of the group— helps to reinforce the importance of the journey rather than focusing solely on the destination.

APPLAUDING ACCOMPLISHMENT

The small accomplishments made during the struggle to create a work, such as developing the concept or putting your ideas on paper, are the stepping stones that propel a writer forward. Acknowledging the small steps reminds the writer that she is making progress.

In the Southern New Hampshire Women's Writing Group, Karen has found that celebrating together is often the only time she has to enjoy her writing accomplishments. "Celebrating a hand written rejection, the mailing of five submissions, the completion of a first draft, or a breakthrough in a writing problem can be best done with people who have been there themselves. When I finished the first draft of a novel, the non-writers in my life wanted to know why it wasn't on its way to the bookstore. But my writing group was able to confirm for me that I was on the right track and had succeeded."

> "Success is never so interesting as struggle—not even to the successful."
> —Willa Cather

Deborah remembers when our group celebrated the publication of her first essay in a national magazine. "I was in Florida visiting my parents when I heard the essay would be published. After sharing the excitement with my husband and family, I contacted the group via e-mail. Everyone's responses helped me to relive the excitement. I knew that the group would know—perhaps more than most other people— just how much this meant to me."

The group's acknowledgment of every success, no matter how small, reinforces that every writer is moving forward with her work.

ENJOYING THE CELEBRATION

In the SNHWWG our best ideas and creative spirits often emerge when we are celebrating. Our hectic lives are left behind, and we are able to reflect on our progress, dream about what is to come, and be silly. Celebrating together deepens the bond between group members, which, in turn, makes everyone feel comfortable to be creative.

We celebrate being writers and living a writing life by picking up small writing-related tokens when we travel. For example, Charlene brought everyone pictures of Hemingway's house from Key West, Martha purchased pens in Hong Kong, and Sue brought erasers from Paris.

There are infinite ways to celebrate within a writing group. Finding creative ways to encourage and inspire one another helps to keep the fun in writing when the going gets tough.

Gathering to celebrate the year's accomplishments. From left, Martha (group member), Sue, Karen, Barbara (group member), Charlene, and Deborah

MAINTAINING MOMENTUM

Every time a writer reaches a milestone in her writing, it gives her the courage to strive for more. Take the monumental task of writing a novel. Viewed as a whole, it can be overwhelming. Yet, when the project is broken into smaller pieces with individual milestones, the prospect of getting to the finish line isn't as daunting.

Laurel was discouraged after she completed the first draft of her novel and realized that several more drafts were necessary. "If it hadn't been for the group's insistence that I had already accomplished a great deal in getting the story on paper, I'm not sure I would have continued. Knowing that there was reason to celebrate just for having completed the first draft encouraged me to tackle the second draft."

Sometimes acknowledgment is warranted when a writer picks up a work after having set it aside for some time. In the SNHWWG members have abandoned works for years at a time because they felt blocked, uninspired, or overwhelmed. Martha had such an experience after completing the first draft of her novel. She was intimidated by the prospect of starting the next draft and took a year off before returning to it. When she resumed work on it, everyone acknowledged her courage and determination to persist by giving encouraging feedback on her submission.

Celebrating the individual milestones reminds the writer that there may be miles to go before she can sleep, to paraphrase poet Robert Frost, but every mile traveled puts her that much closer to her destination.

congratulations, you did it!

Writing is multifaceted. There's the brainstorming stage where a writer gathers ideas. Then there's the actual writing. And the revising. And the writing. And the revising. If a writer wants to get her work published, she must add marketing to her list of tasks. There are so many hurdles along the way that it's easy to get off track or to become discouraged. So why wait until a writer gets her work published to pop the bubbly?

> "Warm fuzzies are part of our writing group as we celebrate anything that resembles success of some sort!"
> —Charlene

In the SNHWWG we find every excuse to celebrate, and no success is too small. Here are some of our favorite excuses for celebrating our accomplishments.

▨ REACHING A MAJOR MILESTONE

Charlene remembers when the group celebrated the completion of the first draft of her first novel, *Dream Street*, and then when the group critiqued the entire novel. "That was a huge milestone for me since I had never really believed I could write a novel." When she went on to receive an "exclusive" from an agency, the group cheered and applauded her accomplishing this major achievement.

▨ PERSONAL ACCOMPLISHMENTS

A writing group helps to put an event in a writer's life into context. For example, when Laurel left her career in the corporate world to become a freelance writer, it was the writing group that understood the enormity of what she had done. She says, "The writing group affirmed my decision every step of the way, assuring me that I wasn't crazy to walk away from my previous career."

There may be less life-altering events that also warrant acknowledgment, such as when a group member reads her work in public. We have gone to hear each other read in bookstores and at writing conferences for moral support and to listen to Barbara sing.

GETTING PUBLISHED

One of the biggest and best reasons to celebrate is when a group member's work is published. When Karen was awarded a contract for a travel guide with a prominent publisher and a monthly column for a newspaper magazine, the group acknowledged these huge accomplishments by presenting her with award certificates. Charlene and Laurel had pieces accepted in the same issue of a journal, which resulted in a celebratory toast. The group especially likes to celebrate collective accomplishments. Sue reflects, "My favorite celebration was for our contract for this book on the first night of our retreat. How exciting—a contract for everyone at the same time!"

how we celebrate

We like to celebrate before, during, and after the creative process to ensure that inspiration follows us on our writing journey. This means we need to be original in our method. After all, a person can only drink so much champagne and still get up the next morning to write. Here are some of our favorite ways to celebrate.

ACKNOWLEDGING EACH OTHER AS WRITERS

First and foremost, we celebrate by recognizing each other as writers. A common salutation in our correspondence with one another is "Dear Sister Writer." This simple greeting reinforces our identity as writers. In the SNHWWG no dream or aspiration is too large or small. For example, one group member might aspire to write a novel while another might simply hope to start writing on a regular basis.

Karen says, "The group celebrates my dream to write full time in many ways, from acknowledging my struggles to helping with suggestions. No one has ever questioned the sanity or validity of that dream. This support bolsters my strength, resolve, and determination."

Sue likes the fact that members really listen when authors are struggling and that they offer both encouragement and advice. "This is very helpful in acknowledging myself as a writer."

Our motto in the SNHWWG is that if we embrace our dreams, we can attain them. So we address each other as sister writers, listen to one another, and continue on our journey.

FEEDBACK DURING GROUP

The feedback we give each other on our work is a primary form of acknowledgment within the group. Charlene says, "Every time I get feedback is so important to me. I am addressed as a writer, by people who know what they're doing, and I always gain from it."

We make a point to acknowledge an author's accomplishments before we give more detailed and constructive feedback. For example, when someone has been struggling with an element of craft or has taken some time between drafts of a work, a group member will congratulate that person for the progress she has made.

E-MAIL COMMUNICATIONS

The most common way we share news with one another is through e-mail. An author might send an e-mail saying that she has had a great writing day or that a work has been accepted for publication. A flurry of e-mails from group members is sure to follow, with celebratory comments and congratulations. Deborah says, "I like the e-mail responses to each other's successes because they are usually the most immediate. They're heartfelt and enthusiastic, with lots of exclamation marks!!!!"

GROUP GATHERINGS

Another favorite method of celebration in the SNHWWG is gathering for special meals. Charlene is fond of the Saturday night during the annual weekend retreat when the group goes out to dinner. "It's always following a day of work, and it feels so luxurious to be out together goofing off and having a nice dinner as writing friends." We also enjoyed an authentic Moroccan dinner that Karen prepared before a regular group meeting.

Our group looks forward to the annual holiday celebration in December, which is usually a potluck affair. One year we brought dishes related to the settings and characters in our novels. Deborah brought Dutch cheeses and crackers to reflect the setting of her novel while Charlene brought stuffed pasta shells to reflect a central character's ethnic heritage. At this holiday gathering, we also reflect on our accomplishments during the previous year.

making your journey a special one

Taking the time to celebrate and acknowledge one another's accomplishments during the journey helps to emphasize the quest rather than the destination. This is important given we can't always predict our destination as writers. We can, however, do everything within our power to enjoy our journey, stopping to smell the ink cartridges along the way.

Ten

Exercises for your Writing Group

You get out of bed—shivering in the cold air—to walk or bike as the sun lazily rises. Why? Because the muscles of your body need exercise to stay healthy, as does your heart and your psyche. We exercise because we feel better when we do, we have more energy, and we are nicer people to be around.

What about writing? Should we use the keyboard as a weight, and pump keys instead of iron? How about flexing your writing hand by twirling your favorite pen around with the sound of Richard Simmons in the background? Sounds silly of course, but your writing brain needs exercise just like other parts of your body. The way to get that exercise is not physical, but mental and creative.

When we exercise as a group we become like a team in training, watching each other's writing muscles grow. We all benefit from each other's increased strength as writers.

benefits of writing exercises

Writing exercises can be used to tighten flab, tone and stretch our writing minds. Sometimes when we sit down to write, with the time scheduled and free of distractions, the page refuses to sprout witty, poetic, and publishable phrases. We can sit and wait, hoping the muse is just busy at a house down the road. Surely she or he will be visiting any minute. Or better, we can take a pro-active approach and start working on writing exercises that will jog the mind. They can help to overcome that dreaded phrase that writer's sometimes can't say out loud—writer's block. Some writers keep the results of their writing exercises in a folder to turn to whenever they need inspiration. A certain word, phrase, character, or image may be just the one they need to be off and running.

Other writing exercises can be helpful if you're having a difficult time with characters who won't fully reveal themselves to you, hiding behind a layer of gauze that obscures their features, or speaking in such whispers that you must strain to hear. Sometimes as the writer, we know clearly how a character will behave in one scene, and then have no clue in another.

Another benefit of a writing exercise is to clarify the plot, particularly of a novel. When working on a novel over a long period of time, it can become difficult to keep the plot points straight and to tell if the story is moving forward.

For any of these writing difficulties, open this book to a writing exercise and work out. After you've used several of them, create your own, or look at books on writing, for additional exercises. Most writers have their favorites, and there are many variations. While many of these exercises in this chapter can be done alone, we have given them a group slant because, after all, that's what this book is about.

stretch your writing mind

We all know that before exercising, it's a good idea to stretch so we can get the full benefit of the workout. Likewise, a good writing exercise can provide a helpful stretch to ready us for some serious writing.

• clustering

This exercise is as simple as jotting a word on a piece of paper or easel and making free associations with the word. Clustering is a great way to unleash creativity, and all you need is a pencil, a piece of paper, and a ready mind. It is ideal to gather the collective ideas of a group in one sitting, and it can be done in an informal atmosphere. The progression of thought is always amazing and can offer unexpected breakthroughs in your writing.

There are a couple of ways you can do this exercise. One person could choose a topic and everyone could do clustering work on the same topic individually, or the group could cluster together simultaneously on the same topic. Have

CLUSTERING

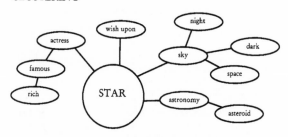

one person document the ideas of the group on an easel so that everyone can see the progression of the exercise. Put a circle around each word, and then draw lines between the words to connect them. See where the clustering takes you.

• *random writing*

This exercise is most fun at a retreat but could be just as easily done at a group meeting. It can be great fun because you are not constrained by your own story or characters. You may be inspired by what someone else has written.

Each group member brings a paragraph that she has already written, perhaps from a short story, essay or poem, and attaches it to a few sheets of blank paper. Everyone is asked to leave these anonymous contributions somewhere in the room or house—like the kitchen, bathroom, or on top of the coffee table. Then everyone has the opportunity to write an additional paragraph on each of the contributions. Group members can add to all of the pieces, or just those pieces they choose as often as they want. The tone can be serious, poetic, or just plain zany. When everyone has written, the person who began the story or essay reads it out loud to the group.

• *round robin writing*

How a writer chooses to begin her work is as different as each writer. This exercise is a good way to look at your own writing process and is an opportunity to learn from others.

Set a timer for two or three minutes, depending on how much time you have for this activity and the number of people participating. Each writer should write for the designated time. When the timer goes off, the writer passes her page to the person on her left and takes the page that is handed to her. Set the timer again and continue writing the story that was handed to you. This exercise works best when you can switch at least three times. When done, share the stories. They'll be fun, will probably take unexpected turns, and you'll learn a lot about yourself as well as each other.

• *two truths and a lie*

Fiction writers face the challenge of convincing their audience to believe something that is not true. This exercise illustrates that truth can indeed be stranger than fiction, and that reality doesn't always work for fiction if the situation is not believable.

Each member should write three short tales about herself; two of these must be true, one must be untrue. Include specific scenes or details. After each group member reads her story, everyone guesses which one is not true. The storyteller reveals the truth after everyone has guessed.

• *"what i really mean to say is..."*

This exercise is inspired by Natalie Goldberg and is most helpful when your writing seems superficial, or you're not certain what you are trying to say. In addition, perhaps members of your group feel the story is unclear.

There are two ways to approach this exercise.

1. *One writer discusses having trouble getting to the point in her writing, or members giving the writer feedback on her work have said they are not sure what the writer is trying to say. All of the group members, including the author, take three to five minutes to write down what they think she is trying to say. Depending on time constraints, everyone*

can hand their writing exercise to the author, or they can all take turns reading it aloud to her.

2. *Begin with a freewrite for ten minutes, then pair up within the group. Each person takes a turn reading her freewrite, then both write for three to five minutes about what they think their partner is trying to say. Again, depending on time constraints, these can be read aloud or given to the writer.*

• words in a paragraph

This exercise is often used in writing workshops and classes to stimulate the brain and get it moving in creative directions.

Someone contributes a list of totally unrelated words; six is a good number to work with. An example would be: ice cream cone, skyscraper, doorbell, blouse, tombstone, and carnival. Any combination is fine. Then, group members take five to ten minutes to write a meaningful paragraph using the list of words. The total unconnectedness of the words is what causes your brainwaves to scramble for a way to relate them. Why not start by using the above list? Ready, set, go!

• write about a group experience

This exercise can have some interesting results, illuminating some of the differences between group members. Sharing what each group member picks up from an experience can help to show the other members what was not immediately obvious to them.

After a group outing, take some time for members to write down what they remember, how they felt, what they saw. Members should include sensory and emotional details as they reflect on their experience. At the end of the exercise, each member has the opportunity to read what she has written. Spend some time looking at the differences between the observations.

• write about an object

As writers, we often need to be able to see things from another's point of view. This exercise is designed to strengthen our ability to do this.

Each member of the writing group focuses on the same object in the room, then writes about that object for five minutes. By sharing our writing, we discover how differently we all see the world.

give those characters definition

Ah, those elusive characters. They create the action in our stories just as muscles do in our bodies. Sometimes we know them like we know ourselves and other times, we have no idea what their favorite brand of underwear is, what they wear to bed, and what they do when no one is looking. Writing exercises that focus on our characters can help bring clarity to their unique personalities.

• characters out of character

It is sometimes difficult to force characters into situations that make you uncomfortable or that don't match with your original intent. However, putting characters into new and sometimes uncharacteristic situations can be illuminating—both for the development of the character and for the story. Since this is hard to do to the characters you have birthed, nurtured, and developed, the group can be a great resource.

Each member should pick a character from another member's work. This can be done by putting the character names on pieces of paper and placing them in a bowl, then choosing a name randomly. Another option is if a member has a particular character she is struggling with, everyone could choose to work with the same character. Write a few paragraphs about that character in an unusual situation, or have the character behave in uncharacteristic ways. Read the pieces aloud and enjoy the results.

• character tirade

Characters become real to the author. They live in our minds and souls. We walk around with them day in and day out, talk to them in our cars, pick out toothpaste for them, and otherwise get to know them. There are times when a character will get on your nerves. Since your writing group is becoming intimately familiar with your characters, they may be feeling the same frustration as you.

Everyone in the group can write about the same character, or choose a different character from their own stories to write about. All members can take some time to "tell-off" the bothersome character. Write everything about the character that is annoying or nerve wracking. Go on a tirade. Don't worry about the character's feelings or the repercussions. Let loose!

• conduct character interviews

What is your character's earliest memory? What is her most embarrassing moment? Favorite food? Music? Clothing? The types of questions that a writing group asks can help authors gain insight into their characters and create background information during the process. The details that come out of an interview may not be used in a final manuscript. The idea is to help authors bring their characters to life and to develop multidimensional people.

To do this exercise, have group members take turns interviewing an author about a particular character in her work. No question is too general, too specific, too silly, or too trite. Have fun helping fellow group members bring their characters to life!

• describe a typical day for a character

Knowing all of the minute secrets that a human being carries around in the course of just one day can help flush out details that contribute to your character's personality in your novel or short story.

Start with one of those characters that you're struggling with, and then visualize a typical day. Freewrite what she did, said, ate, wore, laughed at, cried at, and fought over for that entire day. Who did she leave in bed when the alarm went off, and did she heave the clock across the room or gently tap it to shut off the alarm? What clothes did she put on, how did she fix her hair, did she eat breakfast in the car or on the subway and on the way to what job? Include some dialogue and at least one confrontation to give you a feel for her voice, education, and how she solves relationship problems. Once you've finished, share what you have learned about your character with the rest of the group. It could be submitted to the group for feedback, which would illuminate where you're heading with this character.

• *two characters from different novels meet*

The purpose of this exercise is to put characters created by group members into a different situation from their original story and give them an opportunity to interact with one another.

Within the group, choose two characters from different stories. These should be characters that everyone is familiar with from members' novels or short stories. Either decide as a group or individually where these two characters will meet. Write for fifteen minutes and include dialogue, what the characters are wearing, and how they react to one another. It might be more interesting to take characters who are very different from one another so there is conflict when they meet. Make it bizarre or hilarious. They could meet at a hair salon, sitting on a train, or in a car accident where both think the other is at fault. The setting and source of conflict don't have to be in keeping with the original novel or story. Leave enough time for each member to read her version aloud.

• *zoom in on a character*

Picture yourself as a cameraperson. It is your job to film the story and get close ups at the proper times. Now, get ready to do this with your pen. Group members will handle the change in perspective differently. An added bonus is learning how other group members see our characters or objects important to our stories.

Group members should bring an object from, or a picture of, one of their characters. Take turns placing it in the center of the room. Each writer should stand against the wall. Write a paragraph describing what you see. Walk closer. Write another paragraph from this new perspective. Keep going until you are standing so close you can look directly down on the picture or object. Describe what it looks like from this point of view.

build strong plots

Plots are to our stories what bones are to our bodies. Bones and plots need to be strong enough to support everything else.

• *"a sweeping saga"*

This exercise was first developed at one of our retreats and proved to be hysterical, as well as helpful. The purpose is to summarize the novel or short story that each member is working on.

> *Everyone should bring several novels to a meeting or retreat. If possible, include some romance and historical fiction that involves several generations. Take turns reading the summary on the jacket of the novel aloud. Then take turns writing one or two sentences for the novel or short story that each member is working on. Start the first sentence with "This story is a sweeping saga . . ." These can be handed to the author, but it's more fun and helpful to the entire group to read them aloud. This exercise can help authors determine which primary plot points stand out to others in the group.*

• *group summarizes each other's novels—for query letters*

As if writing a story isn't enough, there comes a time in every author's life when she must promote her work if she wants to share it with an audience. It can be a challenge to describe one's own work, which is why this exercise is ideal to do as a group.

> *Peruse the jackets of popular novels to get familiar with the marketing jargon. This will get your creative juices flowing. Devote a half hour to each group member's novel, describing each story as you would for an agent or publisher. If an author has already drafted a query letter, the group can critique the draft.*

• *plot points on paper*

Plot points are major turning points or scenes in a story or novel. If you need some sense of direction during your first draft, it may help focus you. If, however, you tend to write your way to the end, finding your way as you go, then it may be better suited to a second or third draft.

There are three variations to this activity.

1. *The group can read an already published short story or novel in advance and analyze the plot points.*

2. *Each member chooses her own story or novel and works on this individually, then discusses the results as a group.*

3. *Choose one member's story or novel that all members know well. The entire group can work on this together, discussing the plot points as they go.*

This exercise can be done using poster board, a flipchart, or continuous feed computer paper. You will need plenty of room to write. Use markers to draw a long, straight line and mark the plot points on the line, including the midpoint scene and climax scene. It may also be helpful to add other key scenes that help track where you are in the story.

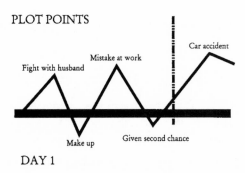

PLOT POINTS

Fight with husband

Mistake at work

Car accident

Make up

Given second chance

DAY 1

• *what if?*

Stumbling blocks can be frequent in the development of plot, and it is sometimes difficult to see all of the possibilities when you are in the middle of it. Group members can help an author work through the blocks and develop plot lines that may not have been obvious.

One member should propose a plot issue or all members can submit ideas on pieces of paper and pick one from a bowl. Write the idea on large paper and tape it to the wall. Brainstorm the possible roads the story line can take from that one situation. Chart the ideas, branching off for all of the various possibilities. Each member should ask "what if," and try to keep in mind the behavior of the characters involved.

keep your writing fit

At the beginning of this book we suggested that a writing group could help you lose twenty pounds, and you might have believed us. Hopefully these writing exercises will help you lose twenty pounds of writer's block. Hey, that's heavy stuff! Exercises will strengthen and tone your writing mind, characters, and plot. That all adds up to becoming a stronger writer.

Charlene Pollano

Working through the heavy stuff with writing exercises.

Eleven

Retreats and
Writing Days

You've been working, writing, meeting, and giving feedback. Now it's time to get away, take a break, and enjoy the finer points of living the writer's life. This is your opportunity to shout from the mountain peaks, bookstores, and restaurant tables—you are a writer!

Retreats, writing days, and artist dates afford groups the opportunity to carry the camaraderie and support of the writing group beyond the working structure of group meetings. More than this, they enable the writing group to delve further into their craft, celebrate their relationship, and bond together in a deeper understanding and commitment. This is the chance for members to go out into the world with the security and support of each other as writers.

retreats of our own

As women, we long for the rare chance to escape the demands of our everyday lives. Imagine getting away to a peaceful condo on a mountainside, surrounded only by the support and laughter of your writing group. Laundry, noisy children, demanding jobs, meal preparation, and housework are nowhere in sight. You are free to sleep late or rise early, sit on the sofa, or take a rejuvenating walk. Now, imagine this weekend filled with discussion

"An aspect I love about our weekend retreats is that we truly retreat from our lives, leaving our homes and responsibilities behind so that we can put all of our energy into our work. It's amazing how much we accomplish and how rejuvenated we feel when returning home."—Laurel

related to writing, group projects, exercises, good food and wine, and the opportunity to shower without children running into the bathroom. How much better can it get?

Laurel says, "At the end of our retreats I always try to hold onto that feeling of focus and inspiration, thinking that if I could bottle it I'd be the most prolific writer around."

The Southern New Hampshire Women's Writing Group began organizing weekend retreats when members became tired of drooling over writing retreats and conferences that were too expensive or too far away to attend. Though we continuously dream about attending the Maui Writer's Conference, year after year, ultimately we prefer designing our own. Alas, no palm trees yet!

the purpose of a retreat

Your writing group may plan a retreat to give its members an excuse to get away, or perhaps you are planning an intensive write-till-you-drop session. Whatever the purpose, group members come together for a personally designed writing conference as peers, without the teacher/student component.

It may be helpful to set aside meeting time to discuss individual group members' goals for the retreat. Identify everyone's expectations and requirements ahead of time. Then, decide on the focus of the retreat, how much work you want to accomplish, and how much you want to relax.

First retreat in White Mountains, 1998. From left, Laurel, Karen, Barbara (group member), Deborah, Martha (group member), Sue, and Charlene.

⚋ HOW LONG SHOULD IT BE?

A weekend away is ideal, but it doesn't have to be a weekend. Depending on the group's needs and goals, a retreat can be a half-day, full-day, two-days, and more. This is based primarily on the availability of group members. While some members may be able to slip away for a couple of days, others will probably have to jump through big hoops, arranging childcare and putting things in order at home. Shorter retreats can be equally enjoyable, rejuvenating, and fruitful.

In the SNHWWG we make our retreats a weekend event, arriving Friday evening and wrapping up after lunch on Sunday. When the location permits, some members choose to arrive early or stay late.

⚋ CHOOSE A DESTINATION

Once the group has decided on the retreat and determined the length, it's time to pick a location. A retreat can be as close as the local library or hours away. However, since part of the reason for a retreat is to get away, it's nice to do just that.

The SNHWWG is based in southern New Hampshire, a couple of hours from the rugged Maine seacoast, the glistening lights of Boston, and the peaceful beauty of the White Mountains. The options for retreat locations are seemingly endless, yet we tend to run for the hills.

When choosing a location, keep the following factors in mind:

- *space for everyone to sleep comfortably if it's more than a day*

- *room to spread out for individual writing time, as well as space to gather together for meals and group activities*

- *activities and facilities available for diversions such as walking, exercising, swimming, and sauna*

- *restaurants within reasonable distance, if the group wants to eat out*

If your group is not comfortable sharing close sleeping quarters, look for a hotel with common areas or nearby facilities to use for group time.

Our group braved a blizzard that dumped eighteen inches of snow, to drive to a retreat in the White Mountains. Sue and Charlene spent over five hours inching along back roads, the snow banks higher than the street signs. Karen and Laurel ended up doing a 360-degree turn in the middle of the highway, landing softly and unharmed in a snow bank. When we arrived, we stopped at the "five and dime" for candles and the bakery for dessert (not necessarily in that order), preparing for the possibility of a power outage. We were determined to have our retreat, nor'easter or not!

Once your group discovers the benefits of a retreat, nothing will stand in your way.

SETTING AN AGENDA

The next step is to decide on an agenda for the weekend, which will depend on where each writer is in her process. Based on the length of the retreat, you can work social, group, and individual time into the agenda. Build in time for meals and exercise as well. And don't forget to check out any bookstores in the area, particularly if there is a discount bookstore close by.

The members of the SNHWWG have taken advantage of the weekend retreats for a variety of reasons: getting back to writing after a long absence, experimenting with new writing ideas, editing and revision work, journaling, and reading. Martha spent one retreat with index cards spread across the floor, trying to reorganize the plot points of her novel. At another retreat, Charlene patched her novel back together after having changed it significantly in an attempt to please an agent. "I probably never would have finished if I had to do it in spurts," Charlene says. "It took hours of concentration and lots of space! I was rejuvenated after the weekend, and also very tired, knowing that I had accomplished a lot. It jump-started me in a big way."

ACTIVITIES FOR YOUR RETREAT

There are a host of group activities for a retreat, limited only by your own imaginations. Try the group writing exercises found in Chapter 10 or discuss inspirational books. Once we had great fun coming up with one-line blurbs for each other's novels. We've also benefited from sharing our favorite novel openings and first lines. Group brainstorming sessions can prove to be quite productive and entertaining.

WHAT WORKS FOR US

The members of the SNHWWG gather for one weekend each year. We try to organize our retreats for the same time of year so that each member can put it on her calendar. We tend to go to the same location, although we don't always stay in the same condo. The familiarity, as well as the destination itself, adds to the ritual and comfort of the retreats. They tend to be work oriented, with agendas—planned well in advance—packed with writing exercises, discussions, and most importantly, time to write on our own. (You can hear a pin drop during these sessions.) They are also filled with social time and exercise.

We plan our meals in advance, each contributing food to share. Bringing meals that are already prepared or quick to assemble ensures that no one spends too much time in the kitchen. We plan one evening meal at a nearby restaurant.

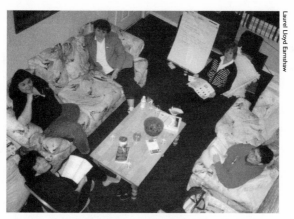

Work session at April 2000 retreat. From left, Deborah, Karen, Sue, Charlene, and Martha (group member).

COST CUTTING TIPS

There are a number of steps your group can take to minimize the cost of a retreat.

- *Look for off-season rates at popular tourist destinations. We plan our trips in the mountains for April, after the ski season, when the rentals are less expensive.*

- *Ask everyone you know if they have a condominium, house, or time-share unit that they rent out to vacationers. If not, maybe they know someone who does.*

- *Bring food rather than go out to eat.*

- *Limit the commute time to decrease the travel costs.*

- *Consider using free facilities, such as libraries and picnic areas.*

- *In the summertime, contact a local college or university, many of which will rent dorm rooms for low rates.*

- *Share dorm-style bedrooms, or bring air mattresses to put on the floor. Sleeping on pull-out couches is also an option.*

artist dates

Artist dates are another great way for group members to gather as writers. Getting together with your sister writers offers the opportunity to plan an outing with a literary theme. There are countless literary related activities available, and who better to do them with than your sister writers? They understand why you swoon over Hemingway's House, insist on your 100th stop at Mark Twain's house, kiss Jane Austen's grave, or touch every surface in Shakespeare's house. Of course, many of these locations are not readily accessible, but there are local options for everyone.

SUPPORTING OTHER WRITERS

What better way to celebrate being writers than to support other authors and get close to some of your favorites? The easiest way to do this is to attend book readings and signings. You are probably already more familiar with your local bookstores than your local lingerie store! Many bookstores sponsor readings and signings to promote new books and favorite authors. This is not only a great chance for your writing group to gather in the ultimate literary setting, but also to talk writer-to-writer with published authors.

The SNHWWG members have commented that after attending readings by well-known authors, they feel rejuvenated and energized. Deborah has twice heard one of her favorite authors, Louise Erdrich, read. "It was a great opportunity to ask a gifted writer questions about her craft and use of metaphor."

As more of your writing acquaintances enter the publishing world, you may have the opportunity to attend publication parties. These are thrilling events that celebrate the arrival of a new book—a sort-of coming out party for the author. Several members of the SNHWWG attended one such event for a writing acquaintance whose first book we had previously critiqued in writing workshops.

✄ CONFERENCES AND WORKSHOPS

Writing conferences are a great activity for a writing group. Members can spend the day discussing writing, working on their own craft, and communing with other writers. If group members attend different workshops at the conference, they can share the information and handouts with those who do not attend. We attend various workshops and come back together to share our booty. Conferences often afford the opportunity for attendees to read aloud, enabling group members to practice public reading with the support of their writing sisters.

One of Laurel's favorite group activities is to attend the New Hampshire Writers' Day. "We hear the keynote speaker together," she explains, "then we branch out to take various classes and workshops during the day. At the open reading, we cheer each other on. Because of the group's support, I have the courage to read my work, knowing that if I collapse from nerves, one of my fellow writing sisters will scoop me up."

"I really believe that I am a writer when I participate in days and weekends devoted to the craft of writing with other women who feel the same way. There are no others who could help contribute to this feeling of accomplishment more than these women."—Charlene

✄ LITERARY SITES

It may require research, but it is likely that there are literary related sites within reach for almost everyone. These can be an author's home, a writer's beloved garden, a park or lake immortalized in poetry, or a town that served as the setting for a favorite book. A trip to the destination may include a picnic lunch and readings that relate to the site.

In New England, we are fortunate to have a bounty of such attractions. There is Walden Pond in Concord, Massachusetts, forever immortalized by Henry David Thoreau. Celia Thaxter's garden on the Isles of Shoals, off the coast of Maine, is a unique and inspiring destination. The Isles of Shoals are also the setting for Anita Shreve's novel *The Weight of Water*. John Irving has set his novels in Exeter and Hampton Falls, New Hampshire. If you're a Jack Kerouac fan, there is a pilgrimage site in Lowell, Massachusetts (not to mention San Francisco, California).

Exploring the literary sites in your area will enrich your writing life. Why not begin your search with your local librarian?

Another activity is to visit locations in members' novels and stories to research the settings. If a group member is writing a novel set in a particular local town, the group could spend an afternoon walking in her character's footsteps and soaking in the details of the scene.

Members of the SNHWWG have spent time in Boston, investigating the Museum of Fine Arts, picking out homes on Commonwealth Avenue, and exploring the North End, to unearth details for Deborah's, Laurel's, and Karen's novels.

> "When I visit literary sites, I feel as though I am connecting with the writers who went before me. I feel part of a larger community and tradition."—Karen

Many writers dream of the day they sell the movie rights to their books. Why not see a movie adapted from a book—particularly one you've enjoyed?

writing days

Writing days give the group a chance to come together to write, focus on the business of writing, and work in depth on craft in a way that can't be done during regular group meetings. Writing days are similar to one-day retreats with the emphasis on writing rather than getting away. This is a less expensive alternative to a full-blown retreat and more manageable than a weekend away. Group members may also encourage each other to take writing days by themselves.

Writing days can take place in any number of locations, from a group member's home to the beach. Local libraries often have conference rooms that provide a perfect literary setting for writing. Outdoor settings are particularly inspiring for many writers. For example, Charlene and Sue feel inspired by the silent camaraderie, as well as the historical surroundings of the Robert Frost Farm in Derry, New Hampshire.

THE PURPOSE REVISITED

Just as with writing retreats, spend some time as a group deciding what the writing day will include and what purpose it will serve. It may be a chance for the group to work on writing exercises or help each other through craft problems. A writing day may focus on an element of fiction, such as plot, especially if a number of members are struggling with similar problems.

ARTIST BUDDIES

Occasionally, a couple of group members may want to team up and help each other achieve writing goals. Artist buddies can identify times to meet outside of the writing group and ways to support each other on a more regular and personal level. For example, members of the SNHWWG have teamed up when struggling with writer's block or moving between drafts.

IN CASE YOU STILL NEED CONVINCING

It can be difficult to find the time, space, and money to be a writer. With a group of one's own, retreats, artist dates, and writing days enable members to help each other live the writer's life. Group members can choose from a variety of literary destinations they would like to explore. This support can help you find the strength and security to proclaim yourself a writer!

Twelve

SECRETS OF OUR SUCCESS

Writing is a spiritual journey with many paths. Although we ultimately must face the blank page in rooms of our own, how we make the journey toward creativity and the writing life is up to us. The destination is important for some, but for many, it's the journey that matters most.

Some writers choose to make the journey alone. Others may take along a map to help guide them. Taking writing courses helps with craft and provides contact with other writers. Some writers choose to enter an MFA program. Others hire coaches and editors to critique their drafts. Some read books on craft and process for self-instruction. In the Southern New Hampshire Women's Writing Group, we use our writing group—a group of our own—as our compass to guide us on the journey.

On a trip of this magnitude, it is easy to get disillusioned, distracted, or lost. After all, it isn't easy to drive across the country alone without the benefit of other drivers to keep you awake, take over the driving once in a while, or read the map to help navigate. Our group provides its members with direction, company, and support throughout the writing journey. And, because we're all women, we don't mind stopping to ask for directions!

a journey of our own

As with any journey, your travel companions, road map, and side trips will enrich the experience. Looking back on what has contributed to the success of our journey, our love of writing and the desire to make this love an integral part of our lives has kept us going.

CHOOSING THE RIGHT TRAVEL COMPANIONS

"This sense of traveling the writing journey with companions is what bonds me to the writing group. After having traveled with my sister writers, I can't imagine traveling alone."—Laurel

When we joined the group, many of us were just beginning to call ourselves "writer," and often only when we were together. Writing as a hobby may have been the original reason for joining a group, but since undertaking this journey, a seriousness of purpose has taken hold. Karen says, "We are all dedicated to being writers and to helping each other become writers."

Choosing the right group is a critical decision as you search for your means of leaving "a room of one's own" to live a more creative life.

DIRECTIONS ALONG THE WAY

A group benefits from having guidelines to help it move through the challenging parts of the journey. Navigators help with the logistics of operating a group. They facilitate decisions about locations, times, length of meetings, and setting goals, which are all important in directing us on our journey. There are several members who organize and disseminate our meeting and feedback schedules, meals for retreats, and goals for the year, keeping us all on the right road.

FEEDBACK WHILE ON THE TRIP

"For me, writing something down is the only road out." —Anne Tyler

Although backseat drivers are not always appreciated, it's critical to have co-navigators and co-pilots as we travel the writing road. A group needs to develop guidelines that incorporate the philosophical, technical and emotional aspects of feedback. As Karen says, "Constructive, educated, thoughtful, sensitive feedback is critical to making a writer, and the lack of it can break a writer."

Deborah feels strongly that even though we may disagree on the proper placement of a comma, or how a character should behave in a story, or on what note the ending of an essay should conclude, we know that the person disagreeing with us has our best interest at heart.

Driving alone is possible, but bringing company along for the ride to help with directions, watch for sharp turns, and point out the views enriches the writer's journey.

INSPIRATION ENRICHES THE SIGHTSEEING

When we travel, we sometimes come across sights that we have never seen before. They inspire us to continue as we enrich our senses with spectacular views of nature. On the writing journey, finding ways to nurture our inspiration is what adds to our view and colors the ride with beauty. Learning how to encourage and inspire each other brings a sense of fulfillment to the creative life. Charlene says, "I watch other members working diligently toward living a truly creative lifestyle, and I am inspired to reach for those heights."

FLAT TIRES AND RUNNING OUT OF FUEL

No trip is perfectly smooth since life itself is full of imperfection. Running out of fuel in today's fast-paced culture is to be expected, but companions on the journey can help refuel, tune up weary engines, and change flat tires. Making a trip alone and facing life as it gets in the way is an option, but why face the superhighway alone? The support of a writing group helps us to navigate around the daily roadblocks to our writing destination. Laurel says, "I'm always amazed at how the dynamic of the group propels the work of individual members forward. When one member feels lost in her writing, or just out of gas, another offers the perfect advice or encouragement to give her direction."

During the writing journey, family and friends may not always understand the need to be on the never-ending trip. Karen says, "Even the most supportive and open family members will occasionally feel pushed aside for time spent with the writing group. Stay true to yourself and your dream will get you and your loved ones to the end of the journey."

ARE WE THERE YET?

A long journey affords the opportunity to discuss, learn, share, and enjoy conversation. The writing journey allows companions to observe another's process, share ideas on craft, and witness one another moving closer toward publication. We compare notes, help each other create characters and settings, develop plots, and give birth to our writing voices. Along with the sharing of knowledge on craft, we watch each other develop our individual writing processes. While publication is not the only destination, the tools that some members use can assist others to reach for this if she chooses.

The changing landscape of the publishing world—with new roads leading to E-publishing and mergers that make publication more difficult—increases the odds of becoming lost in a world that is no longer recognizable. Laurel says, "In a writing group, when a member questions if she'll ever find an audience for her work, another shares a publication tip that results in her work being published."

> "It is never too late to be who you might have been."—George Eliot

ᨆ CELEBRATING EACH DAY'S PROGRESS

After a long day's ride, pulling into the hotel parking lot is a reason to celebrate. Helping each other celebrate the little and big triumphs of the writing journey is also an uplifting experience. The spirit of celebration allows us to look back on where we've been as well as dream about the next leg of our journey. It also reminds us to mark every accomplishment whether large or small. It keeps the writing fun while moving us forward on our journey. We continue to find every opportunity to praise each other for our progress. Sue says, "When the group critiqued my entire novel, it was not only useful feedback, but it was a celebration that my novel was complete."

ᨆ STOPPING TO STRETCH ALONG THE WAY

While on a long journey, it is important to take breaks and stretch those muscles. Writing exercises can help a group keep their writing selves limber and will energize your writing life.

ᨆ TAKING A SIDE TRIP

Sometimes the best way to rejuvenate during a long journey is to take a side trip to an unplanned destination that caters to the need for respite. Weekend retreats and writing days carve space out of a busy life to submerge oneself into the writing world—or a nearby Jacuzzi. Surrounded by fellow members, mountains, oceans, or lakes, you can leave your fast-paced world behind and enjoy the camaraderie of other writers.

paving the way

The creative journey of the SNHWWG members contains some important elements that make the trip as smooth as the path to creativity can be. How do we avoid the frost heaves, the washed out roads, and the detours? We consider our differences a strong asset. Deborah says, "I can depend on group members to use their skills to enhance mine." If nurtured, group differences can transform one-dimensional characters and settings into multidimensional worlds. The key is to foster those differences and make the group a safe place for them to thrive.

As we travel toward more creative lives as artists, we struggle to find resources within ourselves that we may have overlooked. It requires an inner search that can be difficult, and not always understood, by the world around us. Trust and respect for the search for our inner lives is critical to the journey. It seems that all else is dependent on whether both are present within the group. If it is, the journey will proceed on a smoothly paved superhighway. If these two elements are lacking, the journey could be on a dirt road filled with potholes and could lead to a dead end.

"Everyone thinks writers must know more about the inside of the human head, but that is wrong. They know less, that's why they write. Trying to find out what everyone else takes for granted."
—Margaret Atwood

Many published writers say that one must persevere in order to be successful. Author John Updike says, "Don't be thin-skinned or easily discouraged because it's an odds long proposition; all of the arts are." A writing group can help members overcome the roadblocks of discouragement. When a member temporarily forgets why she writes, or receives yet another rejection, she thinks of giving up the writing life. There is always another member who reminds her that writing is part of her soul, rejection is part of the game, and leading a writer's life requires perseverance.

Deborah talks about how important our commitment to writing, to the group, and to each other has become. "We are committed to providing thorough, timely, and caring support to each other in a golden rule of writing. We rarely let each other down."

Charlene adds, "Commitment is driving hours in a blizzard to be together at a retreat. It's critiquing pages and pages of manuscript so a member can advance in her writing. It's organizing your life around meetings and writing time and feedback. Commitment binds us together and propels us forward on the creative journey—riding in First Class!"

Laurel says, "Writing group members show commitment to one another in the smallest of ways. Every time they critique the work of a fellow group member, they show their commitment to that person and her work. When they attend meetings despite their hectic lives, they demonstrate their commitment to the group. The stronger the commitment of the individuals, the stronger the bond will be. The stronger the bond, the farther the group will travel on its journey of creative expression."

> "We're all in this
> together—by
> ouselves."
> —Lily Tomlin

Sue says, "Commitment and perseverance go together in the life of a writer. Commitment brings passion and love to the work, but also a sense of responsibility and a need to write. Perseverance takes that commitment to its extreme. It's writing when you don't have time, or you're not really in the mood."

We talk about the importance of perseverance, but most importantly, we have seen it at work. Deborah and Karen, parents of small children, carve out time from their busy schedules to write. Although Sue would rather write than work on her marketing package, she has persisted and achieved publication. Barbara continues to experiment with different genres to tell her story. When Martha was discouraged after completing her first draft of a novel, she picked it up again. Laurel began the third draft of her novel from a new point of view. Charlene felt overwhelmed after a negative experience with an agent, but didn't give up. Finally, we persevered as a group after we submitted our proposal for this book and remained committed to the project while we waited eagerly to hear from a publisher. The result is the book you hold in your hands.

arriving at the final destination

Do you have a destination in mind on your creative journey? Is it finding an outlet for creative expression? Publication? Being able to write full-time? Charlene says, "Living life more creatively and writing as a way of understanding the world around me are my most important goals. Publication is a wonderful addition, and the possibility of a career built around literature and reading, well . . . that's beyond words."

The SNHWWG has been on a journey of words for almost six years. We haven't always had a detailed map; we've hit a few bumps, gotten lost once or twice, been stopped for speeding, and run out of gas here and there. In spite of all of these events, we are on a journey that has illuminated our lives individually and enriched the group as a whole. Whether we follow a compass toward a destination or consider the journey itself its own reward, we are living a creative life.

Through dark and winding roads, we drive to each other's homes and out-of-the-way restaurants. We gather to have an audience for our writing, to hear kind words of praise and kinder words of criticism. But most of all, we come to say out loud, even if only to each other, "I am a writer."

"Finally, one just has to shut up, sit down, and write."
—Natalie Goldberg

The journey to publication: working on A Group of One's Own.

PART TWO

Group Impact on Craft

Character Development and Dialogue

Cleaning the Slate
A Novel by
Karen Desrosiers

The feedback provided by the writing group had a significant impact on the development of characters in my mystery novel, *Cleaning the Slate*. When I first set out to write the novel, I was very focused on the plot—as is the nature of the genre. The group pushed me to develop my characters more completely, giving them quirks, histories, and fully developed lives. This immediately made the characters three-dimensional, so that they jumped off the page and stayed with the reader after she put the book down. The varied experiences and knowledge of the group were also critical in easing my struggle to polish several characters.

One character, Ron Meskar, was not fully developed. The on-going clash and tension between him and his wife, Detective Carina Meskar, was not clear or believable. In the original draft, I had included details that were inconsistent with the character and omitted information that was necessary for believability.

> *"The thing is," Ron said, "I love you. I just don't care for cops." A forced smile flickered on his face. He picked up his wine, quickly draining the glass.*
>
> *She knew he was trying to make light of it, but both his smile and the joke fell painfully short.*
>
> *"I do love you." Ron picked up her hands, squeezing them gently. "I need you there for me."*
>
> *"I'm always there for you," Carina started. "Of course I support you fully."*
>
> *"As long as it doesn't interfere with your job, you mean. Can you get this case reassigned?"*
>
> *"No, I can't. Even if I could, I wouldn't. I don't believe you're asking me to."*

"I need you available to help me. I wanted to have a dinner party next week. Will you be able to leave this case at work?"

"It's only going to get worse." She stopped, watching his face harden.

The group unanimously agreed that the character's motivations were not clear. He wasn't developed fully enough for the reader to understand the tension between Carina and Ron. Martha, whose daughter was a resident at a Boston hospital, provided a wealth of information about the hierarchy, politics, and motivations within the medical industry. I was able to use this information to build a life for the character, Ron, that satisfactorily explained his issues and motivations.

"The thing is," Ron said, "I love you. I just don't care for cops." A forced smile flickered on his face.

She knew he was trying to make light of it, but both his smile and the joke fell painfully short. She put her empty wineglass on the table and picked up the extra. This is why so many cops have drinking problems, she thought. It isn't the pressure of the job, it's the impact it has on the family.

"I do love you." Ron picked up her hands, squeezing them gently. "A position is opening for Chief of Pediatric Surgery. The director told me today."

"That's fabulous. I know you have a good chance at it." Carina leaned forward, wrapping her arms around him in a tight hug. She held her breath waiting for him to return her squeeze, but he never did.

"I want the job," he said, gently pushing her away. He looked past her, running his thumb over his eyebrow. "There's going to be a lot of entertaining involved, a lot of commitments. I'm going to need you there for me."

"I'm always there for you," Carina started. "Of course I support you fully."

"As long as it doesn't interfere with your job, you mean. Can you get this case reassigned?"

"No, I can't. Even if I could, I wouldn't. I don't believe you're asking me to."

"I'm going to need you to be available if I get this job. I need you to get this job. Will you be able to start doing volunteer work, host parties, attend dinners? Will you be able to leave this case at work?"

"It's only going to get worse." She stopped, watching his face harden.

I could not get the voice and dialect correct for another character—a Greek man. Fortunately, Barbara is familiar with the Greek culture. Not only was she able to provide input on details to make the character and scenes realistic, she helped me perfect the character's voice. Prior to feedback, some of his dialogue looked like the lines below:

Cyril laughed. "I get it. You two are some kinda comedy act. I like it. I just wish you'd done this one at the club."

"I hearda him," Cyril said. "I didn't say I know him. I said I heard of him."

Barbara's feedback helped me transform the dialogue, and thus the character's voice, to be much more believable, as shown below:

Cyril laughed. "I get. You two some kind comedy act. I like. I wish you done at club."

"I hear things," Cyril said. "Didn't say know him. Said hear of him."

Mike, a Texan, and one of the main characters in the novel, was flat and forgettable in my first draft. Descriptions and tags like those below did not draw him clearly for the reader.

Mike sat back. "He was a personal injury lawyer. What could he possibly be working on that would get him killed?"

"Ain't he the funny one," Mike said. He turned toward Ann Marie, introducing himself and Carina "We want to ask you a few questions about Matthew Carey."

He could guess who she was talking to and didn't want to ask her about it.

Input and brainstorming from the group allowed me to assign attributes to the character that brought him to life, as illustrated below:

Mike sat back, putting his cowboy boots on top of his desk with a heavy thud. "He was a personal injury lawyer. What could he possibly be working on that would get him killed?"

"Ain't he the funny one," Mike said. He turned toward Ann Marie, introducing himself and Carina. He hooked his right thumb on the silver and turquoise belt buckle fastened to the front of his hand-tooled leather belt. "We want to ask you a few questions about Matthew Carey."

He could guess who she was talking to and knew asking her about it would be like throwing himself in a rattlesnake pit.

Courage and Honesty

"Giving Thanks"
An Essay by
Laurel Lloyd Earnshaw

A challenging aspect of writing personal essays for me is to be able to say what I want without worrying about the consequences. I write about everyday situations that often involve family members. The difficulty occurs when I worry that the people I write about will cringe when seeing themselves in print. For example, in "Giving Thanks" I wrote about the mishaps my husband and I experienced when hosting the Thanksgiving meal for our families. In the first draft of the essay, I hesitated to specify the substance my sister was smoking and didn't want to name the person who believed my pumpkin pie had caused a bout of food poisoning.

When the writing group saw the essay, they honed right in on these two areas where I was holding back and asked for the details. These are how the paragraphs appeared in the first draft.

My free-spirited sister arrived shortly after this fiasco and, over the meal, we told her what had happened. Thankfully, the turkey was quite good (in fact, my brother believed it was cooked to perfection). I told myself the worst was over. As we sat down to dessert and a video, I took a deep breath. But what was that smell? I walked into the kitchen, and my husband simultaneously met me in the hallway, sniffing. We both looked at the closed bathroom door from which the distinct odor of an illegal substance escaped. Seconds later, my sister emerged, looking quite happy with herself. I was horrified. So much for impressing the in-laws.

> *The phone calls started the next day. A family member didn't feel well and launched a behind-the-scenes investigation to determine what people had eaten. Another family relation, who often suffers from stomach distress, also didn't feel well. My husband couldn't breathe after eating a lunch of leftovers (which we later learned was caused by an allergy to hazelnuts). The only food they had all eaten was the pumpkin pie, so my family relation determined that my homemade pie was the source of the poisoning. If she had asked me, I would have told her that everyone else who'd eaten the pie was just fine.*

I couldn't believe that the group found the exact areas where I had struggled. They insisted that I name the illegal substance because the detail would add to the humor. When I told them that the family member was my mother-in-law, they suggested I mention her by name because everyone loves a good mother-in-law story.

In the end, I took the advice of the writing group because I knew they were right. If I compromised what I wrote every time I worried about what another person would think, I wouldn't be doing justice to myself or my readers. Besides, it was really quite funny when I thought about what had happened.

Here is how the paragraphs of the essay appeared in print.

> *My free-spirited sister arrived shortly after this fiasco and, over the meal, we told her what had happened. Thankfully, the turkey was quite good (in fact, my brother believed it was cooked to perfection). I told myself the worst was over. As we sat down to dessert and a video, I took a deep breath. But what was that smell? I walked into the kitchen, and my husband simultaneously met me in the hallway, sniffing. We both looked at the closed bathroom door from which the distinct odor of marijuana escaped. Seconds later, my sister emerged, looking quite happy with herself. I was horrified. So much for impressing the in-laws.*

> *The phone calls started the next day. My mother-in-law didn't feel well and launched a behind-the-scenes investigation to determine what people had eaten. Another family relation, who often suffers from stomach distress, also didn't feel well. My husband couldn't breathe after eating a lunch of leftovers (which we later learned was caused by an allergy to hazelnuts). The only food they had all eaten was the pumpkin pie, so she*

determined that my homemade pie was the source of the poisoning. If she
had asked me, I would have told her that everyone else who'd eaten the pie
was just fine.

When my sister read the piece, her reaction was that she had no idea I
had known about her smoking pot in the bathroom. I told her about my
dilemma in mentioning the particular details, and she said it definitely
made a better story to add it.

I was so nervous about my mother-in-law's reaction to the piece that I
hid the newspaper in which it appeared when I saw it displayed on a coffee table at a family gathering.

This balance between telling a good story and withholding certain details
continues. Need I say that my husband wasn't thrilled when I wrote about his
"Garage Attachment Syndrome or GAS" in a recent essay? After years of
being the focal point of numerous stories, he found a clever way to retaliate:
he started writing a column of his own in which I'm a frequent visitor!

Endings and Believability

"The House Sitter"
A Short Story by
Deborah Regan

One of the elements of writing that I have the most difficulty with is creating credible endings that accomplish what endings are supposed to
accomplish: show an epiphany, make meaning of the story, and remain consistent with the character's personality and story line. Although I rely on
the members of the SNHWWG for many forms of assistance, I most count
on them to guide me to an ending.

In my short story, "The House Sitter," Lily is a professional house and
pet sitter who snoops around the home of her wealthy clients, Bradley and
Monica. Lily is attracted to Bradley and dislikes the condescending Monica
and her nasty cat, Margaret. Lily's snooping reveals love letters to Monica,
hidden in classic novels and signed by the mysterious "G." In my first draft,
Lily calls Bradley in England to tell him that one of the cats is sick and
convinces him to return home.

Feedback from the group indicated they didn't believe that Bradley would return from England because of a sick cat. They also felt that the story was more about the relationship between Monica and Lily, yet the ending was focused on Bradley and Lily.

> *After dinner, Lily removed the three books from the bookcase and laid them on the coffee table like props in a play. She would wait until Bradley had seen Margaret and they had discussed her health. Then she would pour two glasses of VSOP cognac and discuss their similar interests. The final act in her play would be to show him the love letters. Then the green silk lingerie that was hidden beneath her dress would fall to the floor like the final curtain.*
>
> *To pass the time until Bradley arrived, she perused the bookcase for a new book and found one titled The War of the Roses. Hadn't Monica said something about that, something to do with the cats' pillows? She skimmed the book, looking for the cats' names— Margaret and Elizabeth. She found Queen Margaret, "married to King Henry IV, of the House of Lancaster." Farther down, she found Elizabeth Woodville, "a woman of low birth who had married King Edward IV of the House of York." How odd that Monica, who seemed very status conscious, would name her cat for a queen of much higher birth than Bradley's.*
>
> *Suddenly, Lily slammed the book shut. She had behaved like a fool. The house and its belongings were Monica's, not Bradley's. Car lights swept across the driveway and shined through the library window, illuminating the corner where she sat and casting shadows throughout the rest of the room. She heard voices and a door slam, then the key turn in the lock. She buttoned the top buttons on her blouse and picked up the three books to return them to the bookcase that now sat in a shadow.*

The group didn't understand the significance of the cats in relation to the English queens. They also thought Lily was attracted to Bradley for reasons other than wealth, yet the ending made it look like she was scheming to get his money. In the second draft, I rewrote the ending with the focus on Lily seeking revenge on Monica. Lily used Monica's sick cat, Margaret, to aid and abet her. It also includes a new scene with Geoffrey, the gardener, whom Lily had determined was having an affair with Monica. When Margaret vomits, Lily cleans it up with Monica's silk lingerie, and then places it in her dresser drawer. She types a love letter to Geoffrey, telling him to look in the lingerie drawer for a token of her affection, then types Monica's name at the end and places the note in the greenhouse. When Geoffrey arrives, she tells him she's about to go out for a walk.

Lily shut the front door loudly, and then tiptoed up the stairs to the master bedroom. She hid in the closet, keeping the closet door slightly ajar so she could be an audience to the play she had so cleverly directed.

In a few minutes, Geoffrey arrived in the doorway to the bedroom without making a sound on the stairs. He must be used to sneaking around and probably knew every creak on the stairs. He opened the top drawer of Monica's dresser and pulled out the turquoise teddy that lay on the top and held it in his arms. Then the smell hit him.

"What the..." he shouted, throwing the lingerie on the floor. "A token of your feelings, huh? You witch! I should have known it would come to this." He stomped out of the room, and she heard his heavy steps on the stairs.

Lily bit down hard on her finger to keep from laughing. Once she heard his truck start up, she left the closet, laughing hysterically. Before she could walk downstairs, the phone rang.

"It's Monica. What's the problem with Margaret?"

Before Lily could answer, Monica continued, her voice laced with disgust.

"Some professional pet sitter! You can't even handle two little cats," she said, her voice sounding like a cat's hiss.

"Everything's under control," Lily said, grinning as she sprawled on the bed. The sound of Geoffrey's truck screeching as it backed down the long driveway made her suppress a laugh. "I think Margaret knows her place now. In spite of her behavior, I've been enjoying myself, reading the old classics in your library. They're a lot racier than I remember."

Lily paused for effect, but there was no reply. "By the way, you better start looking for a new gardener. That Geoffrey has no sense of humor."

The stunned silence on the other end was the sweetest sound Lily had heard in a while. After she hung up, she picked up the turquoise teddy that Geoffrey had dumped on the floor, took it downstairs and put it in the trash. Margaret glared at her in silence when she walked past her. Lily returned to the bedroom, opened a lingerie drawer and began holding each garment up to herself in the mirror, smiling.

The group liked this ending much better and felt that it fit both the story line and Lily's quirky character. While Monica held the power in her relationship with Lily at the beginning of the story, with the new ending, the reverse was true. The new ending was more believable and more satisfying as a result.

Plot Development and Point of View

No Goodbyes
A Young Adult Novel by
Susan Wereska

My novel, *No Goodbyes*, is about a teenage girl who is abducted by her mother because of a custody dispute. Throughout the entire first draft I struggled with the complex relationship between character and plot, knowing that I wanted to weave the father's search for his daughter into the story. In the first draft, the father's point of view was introduced in the third chapter with a scene showing a discussion between the father and his lawyer.

> *Douglas slammed the stack of papers against the table in the lawyer's office. "What good is all this paperwork if I don't know where she is, Steve?"*
>
> *The middle aged lawyer looked up at his client. He spoke slowly. "Calm down. Getting upset won't help find her."*
>
> *Douglas paced the width of the small office. "I can't calm down. I can't even sit down. I've waited for over a year to be able to see my daughter, and now I can't find her. I went to the house again last night." He stopped to adjust his wire frame glasses. "I've been there every night since the judge announced that I wasn't guilty. Here are the papers reinstating my visitation rights, but no one has been at the house for over a week. How can I calm down?"*
>
> *"Let me get you a cup of coffee." Steve continued to speak in his slow, deliberate manner as he prepared two cups. "Let's look at the facts. We know that you and Casey were divorced seven years ago. You had been married for eight years."*

He handed the cup to Douglas. "You got married after Casey graduated from nursing school but you were still in medical school. She worked at the hospital to help you finish."

He stopped to sip his coffee. "Two years later your daughter, Lauren, was born. After you graduated you opened your dental practice. The following year you and Casey divorced because of all the arguing. Lauren was six then, am I right?"

Douglas sat down and nodded his agreement. "I thought that once the divorce was final things would be better. But Casey never seemed to get over it. We've been fighting over money and Lauren's custody for years. Poor Lauren has always been caught in the middle."

Feedback from group members was that the chapters from the adult point of view would not be of interest to young adolescent readers, and that those chapters slowed the action down. The group members' questions helped me clarify the motives of my characters and resulted in the father being introduced through the eyes of the protagonist's young friends. On-going e-mail dialogue between the friends and the father lets the reader know about his efforts from an adolescent point of view without slowing the action. When Lauren and her mother disappear again, the young friends search the Internet to find her. Since neither of them has a computer at home, they decide to use the computer lab at school.

Mary Lou cast a warning glance at her friend, then typed "MISSING CHILDREN" next to the search command. She held up fingers crossed for luck. "I hope this works. Trying to find Lauren on the Internet was the best lunch time idea you've ever had." Mary Lou typed Lauren Hart on the screen.

A computer message came up. "No matching data," Cindy read. "Try Hartz."

An image of a young Lauren slowly appeared on the screen.

"There it is! That must be an elementary picture," Mary Lou exclaimed.

"Wow. This is great!" Cindy whispered, dancing around the room. "See what it says. Who to contact,"

"Here's an e-mail address" Mary Lou pointed to the screen. And, here's a phone number."

"Douglas Hartz. Must be her father. You were right about the z."
Cindy said, as she copied the phone number. She put the pencil away.

Cindy's scream shattered the silence.

A janitor had entered the room unnoticed. "What are you girls doing in
here?" He spoke sternly.

Mary Lou froze.

"We're working on an extra credit project," Cindy said.

"The principal is still in the building. You'll be talking to her." The
custodian reported them to the office on his walkie talkie.

Minutes later the two girls were seated in the principal's office,
explaining what had happened. They sat silently while she opened a file
cabinet and read one of the files. Then she picked up the phone and looked at
Cindy. "Could I have that number for Douglas Hartz?" she asked.

Cindy handed her the paper she had written on. The principal dialed,
then turned on the speaker phone. After several rings, they heard an
answering machine tape. This was interrupted by a man's voice answering
the phone.

The principal introduced herself and asked if he was the father of
Lauren Hart.

"I have two girls in my office who say they are friends of your
daughter. They knew Lauren during the six weeks she attended school here.
Today they stayed after school and found your web page, which is how
we got your phone number."

"I have a daughter, Lauren Hartz. She has been missing since
September. Do you have information about her?" He paused, then
continued. "When did Lauren go to school there?" His voice sounded far
away, as if he was talking into a tin can.

"In the fall. We were on the gymnastics team together," Cindy drawled.

I saved a note that Lauren wrote to me on the first day of school. She
wrote that her last name was Hartz and she was from Connecticut, but
later, her mother said they were from Boston and that their last name was
Hart. We didn't think much about it until she disappeared." Mary Lou
continued the story.

"Disappeared? What do you mean, disappeared?" The girls could hear worry in the father's words.

"Well, we were all supposed to go to a gymnastics meet on a Saturday and there was a dance the night before, so we were all going to the dance and then we were going to sleep over at my house," Cindy shouted into the speaker phone. *"My Daddy was going to take us to the gymnastics meet the next day, but Lauren never came to the dance. We thought she was sick and we couldn't call her because she didn't have a phone. When she didn't come to school for the whole next week, me and my Daddy drove over to her apartment, but there was no one home. We checked with the landlord a couple of times after that but no one ever saw them again."* She leaned back in the chair.

Mary Lou sat forward to speak. *"My Mom and I checked a couple of times too. The landlord rented the apartment to someone else after about a month, but the last I knew, he still had their stuff in his garage."*

The man's voice boomed out of the speaker. *"This is really good news! I'm so glad you called. Great news! The best I've had! Can you give me your phone numbers and addresses? I'm going to come down there to talk to you in person. I want to visit the landlord where Casey and Lauren were living. Maybe they left a clue about where they went."*

Cindy and Mary Lou looked at each other and grinned. They knew Lauren's Dad was smiling five hundred miles away.

Structure and Voice

Dream Street
A Novel by
Charlene Pollano

In my novel, *Dream Street*, I was presented with three issues of craft: finding the voice of twelve-year-olds, determining my audience, and using the right structure to tell the story.

The original structure began with a prologue in which the protagonist looked back thirty years to an event she witnessed in 1963. The rest of the novel took place primarily in 1963 with two twelve-year-old narrators. There was a secondary plot consisting of several chapters in the present, in which the now middle-aged protagonist tried to make sense of her childhood experience. It presented a problem in that the story is about sexual abuse, thereby rendering it inappropriate for young adult readers, even though the story is told in a twelve-year-old voice.

Carly's eyes were the first ones that my bulging eyeballs connected with. They were so large in her small face that she looked startled, like a deer come face to face with the barrel of a shotgun. They were as dark brown as they could be before they would slip into black, but what caught my attention was the wink she gave me as she tried to keep a straight face. I remember my first thought about her. I wanted to be like her.

"Come on over to my house after school," she whispered during catechism. "You can meet my friends."

It was that simple for her. For me, it was like taking a giant step into another planetary system not knowing if the air was safe to breathe. Up to that point in time, the neighborhood kids and my brothers made up my world of playmates, but they were not who kept me from being lonely. My truest friends were the characters in the books I read. I spent long summer days with Scout, Dill and Jem, then Heidi and Grandfather, and finally, Nancy Drew.

They were my role models, right down to physical appearance. My waist-length, auburn pigtails and freckled face were—I thought—just like Anne's in Anne of Green Gables. Only this imagined likeness got me through the Saturday night ritual of shampooing, which consisted of much whining. It wasn't the actual washing in the kitchen sink that caused the ruckus, but the comb out that was the source of pain.

"I gotta go home first and ask my mother," I said to Carly, as I looked at her short, cropped, dirty-blond hair with envy. After school, I watched her hop on a beat-up boy's bike and zip down the street. As she gained speed, she let go of the handlebars and rode no-hands until she disappeared behind a chain of goldenrod schoolbuses.

That day was the beginning of our friendship, as well as the ending of the old me.

The group was invaluable in helping me find an effective structure to tell the story that would make it appealing to adults. With their encouragement,

I tried different points of view and finally landed on a structure that worked. The group also picked up discrepancies in voice, when I inadvertently slipped out of the voice of a child.

I changed every other chapter to third person point of view. These chapters take place in the past with the child narrator. The other chapters— set in the present—are told in first person point of view by the adult narrator who looks back on her past trauma and attempts to bring closure to it. With group feedback, the novel became a combination of a coming of age story as well as an adult story about the power of guilt in a woman's life.

> *While driving to Newcastle, the need to see friends conquers the insistent desire for isolation. It concerns me that I am pushing them away, but I'm afraid they'll see the tremor in my hands, the frightened look now frozen on my face. Three months have raced past since we last met. . . .*
>
> *"For Christ's sake, Nettie, you look like shit!" Lydia says, lowering her rhinestone-trimmed glasses to the edge of her nose.*
>
> *"Would you let me sit down before you start on me?" I say, glancing at the two tables of diners who are now more interested in my appearance than their boiled lobster dinners.*
>
> *"Hi, Nettie," Georgia says, pushing into the booth and hugging me tight to her. "I think you look fine, and I've already ordered your margarita, so sit down and relax. I don't think I've seen you in three months. Where've you been?"*
>
> *"Jesus, Georgia, don't ask her that, we won't see her for another three months!" Lydia chuckles. She takes a drag of a long, slim cigarette and follows it with a swig of Heineken, then reaches over and smoothes the collar of my dress and adjusts my jacket.*
>
> *"Is that your alcoholic beverage of the month?" I say, pointing to the mug of beer. "And by the way, how did you manage to raise three children as nice as yours with a mouth like that?" I laugh. I slide into the booth and feel myself physically settling into the comfort these long-time friendships wrap around me like a thick, wool blanket.*

PART THREE

Resources

The Southern New Hampshire
Women's Writing Group

MISSION STATEMENT

Established in 1996, the Southern New Hampshire Women's Writing Group is dedicated to encouraging women to write and publish their writing.

Each member agrees to:

1. Write regularly.

2. Submit writing to the group for feedback on a scheduled basis.

3. Encourage each other to write.

4. Give written and verbal feedback on submissions, in accordance with feedback guidelines.

5. Attend meetings regularly.

6. Define and review quarterly goals.

Group Mission Statement

Southern New Hampshire Women's Writing Group Membership Guidelines

Membership in our writing group includes three main elements. Members attend meetings, submit work, and provide feedback to other members. We adhere to the following guidelines for our meetings.

1. A schedule for meetings is set during the last meeting of the calendar quarter.

2. Generally, we meet every two weeks and (whenever possible) on the same week night for the entire quarter.

3. At the time we set the schedule, members sign up for feedback times. There are three feedback times at each meeting.

4. Submissions for feedback are due at the meeting previous to when the feedback is scheduled. Work should be submitted no later than the Thursday before the scheduled feedback meeting to allow members time over the weekend to complete the feedback. If the member scheduled to submit is delayed, but still intends to submit, she may notify members by Thursday that they should expect to receive her submission on Friday. If the member who is scheduled for submission is unable to submit, this gives members sufficient time on Friday to arrange for a substitute submission from another member.

5. Meetings are scheduled to last two hours.
   - During the summer, meetings are scheduled from 7 to 9 p.m.
   - During the remainder of the year, meetings are scheduled from 6 to 8 p.m.

6. Meetings are held at "casual" restaurants or members' homes on a rotational basis. These are scheduled with driving distance in mind and we try to alternate east and west locations.

7. Whenever possible, we arrive at restaurants fifteen minutes before the scheduled starting time if we wish to order and eat dinner before and/or during the meeting.

8. At the time we set the schedule, one member is assigned as the group leader for each meeting. She is responsible for the following:

   - starting the meeting no more than ten minutes after the hour, regardless of whether all members are present.
   - ensuring that feedback is completed during the meeting time
   - setting time limits for feedback and giving a "one more minute" warning if time is running short
   - taking brief meeting notes
   - transcribing and distributing meeting notes via e-mail to all group members

The Southern New Hampshire Women's Writing Group

FEEDBACK GUIDELINES

The purpose of feedback is to encourage the writer by recognizing the successful writing techniques she has used, and to use questions and suggestions to strengthen areas that may need improvement. Feedback should always be given honestly, sincerely, and with respectful sensitivity.

Our group uses the following guidelines:

1. Work submitted may be up to twenty pages in length, double spaced, and may be accompanied by focus questions from the author.

2. Each reader should respond with a minimum of one written page to be shared orally at the meeting. This oral sharing time should be uninterrupted, since each person will get a turn to respond to the piece.

3. The group leader may set time limits depending on other agenda items.

4. Authors may request a specific type of feedback, for example, oral reading followed by discussion, open discussion about a certain topic, or general discussion on a completed lengthy piece.

5. Feedback should begin and end on a positive note. It may include such elements as references to plot, character, pace, tone, mood, theme, grammar, line editing, language, imagery, and potential publishers. Recommended reading may also be used to reference an element in the submitted piece.

6. When giving written and oral feedback, the author should be referred to as the "narrator" rather than directly as "you" to help the author maintain distance from her work.

Group Feedback Guidelines

Karen Desrosiers
Writing Mission Statement
January 1, 2002

➢ To become a full-time writer
➢ To publish in multiple genres, including mainstream fiction, mystery, juvenile fiction and non-fiction, travel, and non-fiction
➢ To write and market a screenplay

Goals for accomplishing Mission

#1 - *A Group of One's Own*
a. Assist in writing and editing
b. Complete sketches for visuals
c. Assist in marketing

#2 - *Daytrips*
a. Finish *Daytrips Quebec* and review final proofs
b. Query for *Daytrips Ontario* and *Daytrips Atlantic Provinces*
c. Query for *Family Daytrips*

#3 - *Cleaning the Slate*
a. Finish final draft
b. Continue marketing
c. Begin writing as a screenplay
d. Market screenplay

#4 - Articles and Short Stories
a. Continue marketing mystery short story
b. Write and market articles for Quebec
c. Finish and market articles for Ireland
d. Finish and market Calistoga, CA article

FEEDBACK SCHEDULE
(Quarter Two 2001)

RECEIVE FEEDBACK on April 12 at Lakeside (Please mail or e-mail)

1. Laurel
2. Barbara
3. Martha

SUBMITTING: Martha, Sue, Karen   Leader: Charlene

RECEIVE FEEDBACK on April 26 at Loaf and Ladle

1. Martha
2. Karen
3. Sue

SUBMITTING: Karen, Sue   Leader: Karen   Absent: Cyndy

RECEIVE FEEDBACK on May 10 at Lakeside

1. Karen
2. Karen
3. Sue

SUBMITTING: Cyndy, Barbara, Charlene   Leader: Martha

RECEIVE FEEDBACK ON May 24 at Loaf and Ladle

1. Cyndy
2. Barbara
3. Charlene

SUBMITTING: Cyndy, Martha, Deborah   Leader: Sue   Absent: Martha

Meeting and Feedback Schedule

Nonfiction Editor
New England Review
Middlebury College
Middlebury, Vt 05753

To Whom It May Concern:

I ask you to consider that there are few people in this world who can boast that a bathtub had a profound effect on them that lasted a lifetime. The enclosed creative nonfiction piece, "The Ladies' Bathtub," tells such a tale.

The setting for this story about a young girl's "coming of age" is a naturally formed swimming hole in the Pemigewasset River in Lincoln, New Hampshire. We all remember those moments in our lives when we had to leave behind the old way of "being" in favor of the new. The protagonist in this story accomplishes just that, with a little help from a Native-American ghost and, to her chagrin, none from the older brother that she idolized. As a professional counselor working with adolescents in the school setting, I am confronted daily with the need in people to come to an understanding of the influences, both good and bad, on their lives.

I believe that "The Ladies' Bathtub," a story about challenge and change, is a metaphor for the town of Lincoln which serves as the setting, and in many ways, as the main character.

For the past five years I have taken numerous creative writing courses and have received coaching from a published author and freelance editor. I am also a member of a writing group that has met biweekly for three years.

Thank you for any time and consideration you may give "The Ladies' Bathtub." I look forward to hearing from you.

Sincerely,

Enc: "The Ladies' Bathtub"
     SASE

Cover Letter

April 6, 2001

Mr. Earl Steinbicker
Hastings House
Eagle Publishing Corp.
9 Mott Avenue
Suite 203
Norwalk, CT 06850

Dear Mr. Steinbicker,

While perusing your web-site I noticed that Hastings House has not yet published *Daytrips* guides for any of the Canadian provinces. Canada is a popular travel destination for Americans and Canadians alike. The Eastern provinces offer European-like culture, breathtaking scenery and unforgettable adventure that are affordable and accessible. Quebec and New Brunswick, Nova Scotia, and Prince Edward Island are ideal candidates for the *Daytrips* series travel guides. I have developed and included possible outlines for both of these guides.

I am an avid traveler, having grown up moving around the United States in a military family. I have spent much of my adult life traveling around the U.S. and Canada, as well as frequent trips to Europe. Preferring to travel independently, and subscribing to the "home base" approach of travel, I have had several occasions to use *Daytrips* travel guides and find them to be an asset to each trip.

My passion for travel is rivaled only by my passion to write. I write essays, travel articles, and fiction. An essay, titled "Routine Kisses", was published in the August 2000 edition of *Parenting New Hampshire*. I am writing a novel and working on a series of travel guides for children. I am a member of the New Hampshire Writer's Project and the Southern New Hampshire Women's Writing Group.

Thank you for your time and consideration in this matter. I look forward to hearing from you.

Sincerely,

Karen A. Desrosiers

Enc: Outlines: *Daytrips Quebec* and *Daytrips Atlantic Provinces*

Query Letter

Publication Credits

LAUREL LLOYD EARNSHAW

Granite Sports Magazine, Summer 2001
    The Making of a Mountain Bike Enthusiast

Journey of Words: Southern New Hampshire Women's Writing Group Anthology, Spring 2001
    Giving Thanks
    My Husband's Garage Attachment Syndrome

Northern New England Review, Fall/Winter 2000
    Tomato Soup Under the Tree and Other Traditions

Our Times Magazine
    Getting Past That Moment
    My Husband's Garage Attach Syndrome (November 2000)
    Longing for a Vampire-Free World (October 2000)
    Out with the Marbles, In with the Gems (March 2000)
    Tomato Soup Under the Tree and Other Traditions (November 2000)

Portsmouth Herald, Special Sections
    Garden Expansion Leads to Life Lessons (Spring 2000)
    Giving Thanks (November 2000)
    How to Be a Mountain Biking Enthusiast (May 14, 2000)
    Move Over White Rice; The Supergrains Are Here (May 19, 2000)
    Wanna Try My Healthy Brownies? (February 11, 2000)

Funny Stuff, No. 7, June 1996
    Longing for a Vampire Free World

Hysteria Magazine, Issue 8, Spring 1995
    Getting Past That Moment

A Library of Our Own

RECOMMENDED READING

Aronie, Nancy Slonim. *Writing from the Heart: Tapping the Power of Your Inner Voice*

Berg, Elizabeth. *Escaping into the Open: The Art of Writing True*

Bernays, Anne, and Pamela Painter. *What If? Writing Exercises for Fiction Writers*

Block, Lawrence. *Spin, Spin Me a Web: A Handbook for Fiction Writers*

Bly, Robert W. *Secrets of the Freelance Writer*

Brande, Dorothea. *Becoming a Writer*

Browne, Renni, and Dave King. *Self-Editing for Fiction Writers*

Bunnin, Brad, and Peter Beren. *The Writer's Legal Companion*

Burgett, Gordon. *Sell & Resell Your Magazine Articles*

Burnham, Sophy. *For Writers Only*

Burroway, Janet. *Writing Fiction: A Guide to Narrative Craft*

Cameron, Julia. *The Artist's Way: A Spiritual Path to Higher Creativity*

Cameron, Julia. *The Right to Write: An Invitation and Initiation into the Writing Life*

Cameron, Julia. *The Vein of Gold: A Journey to Your Creative Heart*

Canfield, Jack, Mark Victor Hansen, and Bud Gardner. *Chicken Soup for the Writer's Soul*

Chiarella, Tom. *Writing Dialogue*

Collier, Oscar, with Frances Spatz Leighton. *How to Write and Sell Your First Novel*

Cool, Lisa Collier. *How to Write Irresistible Query Letters*

DeSalvo, Louise. *Writing as a Way of Healing: How Telling Our Stories Transforms Our Lives*

Dibell, Ansen. *The Elements of Fiction Writing Series—Plot*

Dillard, Annie. *The Writing Life*

Egri, Lajos. *The Art of Dramatic Writing*

Forster, E. M. *Aspects of the Novel*

Gardner, John. *On Becoming a Novelist*

Gardner, John. *The Art of Fiction: Notes on Craft for Young Writers*

Goldberg, Natalie. *Wild Mind*

Goldberg, Natalie. *Writing Down the Bones*

Golub, Marcia. *I'd Rather Be Writing*

Hall, Oakley. *How Fiction Works*

Hall, Oakley. *The Art and Craft of Novel Writing*

Heffron, Jack, editor. *The Best Writing on Writing*

Heffron, Jack. *The Writer's Idea Book*

Hood, Ann. *Creating Character Emotions*

Huddle, David. *The Writing Habit*

Joselow, Beth. *Writing Without the Muse*

Kiernan, Kathy, compiler. *Mark Twain on Writing and Publishing*

King, Stephen. *On Writing: A Memoir of the Craft*

Kress, Nancy. *The Elements of Fiction Writing Series—Middles & Ends*

Lamott, Anne. *Bird by Bird: Some Instructions on Writing and Life*

Lerner, Betsy. *Forest for the Trees: an Editor's Advice to Writers*

Maass, Donald. *Writing the Breakout Novel*

Madden, David. *Revising Fiction: A Handbook for Writers*

Maisel, Eric. *Fearless Creating*

Meredith, Robert C., and John D. Fitzgerald. *Structuring Your Novel From Basic Idea to Finished Manuscript*

Murray, Donald M. *A Writer Teaches Writing*

National Book Award Authors. *The Writing Life: A Collection of Essays and Interviews*

Novakovich, Josip. *Fiction Writer's Workshop*

O'Conner, Patricia T. *Words Fail Me: What Everyone Who Writes Should Know About Writing*

Perkins, Lori. *The Insider's Guide to Getting an Agent*

Perry, Susan K. *Writing in Flow*

Ray, Robert J. *The Weekend Novelist*

Rhodes, Richard. *How to Write Advice and Reflections*

Rico, Gabriele Lusser. *Writing the Natural Way*

Romano, Tom. *Clearing the Way: Working with Teenage Writers*

Rubie, Peter. *The Everything Get Published Book*

Rule, Rebecca, and Susan Wheeler. *Creating the Story*

Shaughnessy, Susan. *Walking on Alligators: A Book on Meditations for Writers*

Sternburg, Janet, editor. *The Writer on Her Work*

Sternburg, Janet, editor. *The Writer on Her Work Volume II*

Strunk, William, and White, E.B. *The Elements of Style*

Thiel, Diane. *Writing Your Rhythm*

Tobias, Ronald. *Twenty Master Plots, and How to Build Them*

Ueland, Brenda. *If You Want to Write: A Book About Art, Independence, and Spirit*

Watts, Nigel. *Writing a Novel and Getting Published*

Woolridge, Susan Goldsmith. *Poemcrazy*

Writer's Digest. *Handbook of Magazine Article Writing*

Writer's Digest. *Handbook of Novel Writing*

Zinsser, William. *On Writing Well: An Informal Guide To Writing Nonfiction*

Our Personal Favorites

"The only advice I give young writers is something
that is alarmingly new to some of them; that is to read.
It never occurs to them. I say, 'If you love to write,
how can you miss what has been written?
How can you do without that great pleasure. . . ?'"
—*Eudora Welty*

✍ Barbara's Favorites

"These books captured my imagination at different stages of my life. As a child, I loved *Dr. Doolittle* and *Pippi Longstocking*, but my favorite was *Charlotte's Web* by E.B. White. As a learner in college, I took my academics seriously and fell under the spell of Colette, Henry James, Thorstein Veblen, and E.B. White's essays. As an adult, I found myself having greater access to women writers. There didn't seem to be as many women's voices as I was growing up. Now there are many rich voices!"

- ✍ Colette. *Earthly Paradise*
- ✍ De Bernieres, Louis. *Corelli's Mandolin*
- ✍ Hamilton, Jane. *Map of the World*
- ✍ Hurston, Zora Neale. *Their Eyes Are Watching God*
- ✍ Ivins, Molly. *Molly Ivins Can't Say That, Can She?*
- ✍ James, Henry. *Portrait of a Lady*
- ✍ Lipman, Elinor. *Then She Found Me*
- ✍ Marquez, Gabriel Garcia. *Love in the Time of Cholera*
- ✍ Redd, Louise. *Playing the Bones*
- ✍ Veblen, Thorstein. *Theory of the Leisure Class*

ℰ *Charlene's Favorites*

"When I was eight, my grandmother enrolled me in a book club. A new book arrived in the mail each month. When it arrived, my mother had strict instructions to find me wherever I was. I would run home from the ball field or a friend's house as if my pants were on fire and devour the book in one sitting. My appetite for reading hasn't changed much since then."

- ℰ   Allison, Dorothy. *Bastard Out of Carolina*

- ℰ   Atwood, Margaret. *Cat's Eye*

- ℰ   Berg, Elizabeth. *Range of Motion*

- ℰ   Bronte, Charlotte. *Jane Eyre*

- ℰ   Carr, Mary. *The Liar's Club*

- ℰ   Hamilton, Jane. *The Book of Ruth*

- ℰ   Hoeg, Peter. *Smilla's Sense of Snow*

- ℰ   Kingsolver, Barbara. *The Bean Trees*

- ℰ   Miller, Sue. *The Good Mother*

- ℰ   Ondaatje, Michael. *The English Patient*

- ℰ   Quindlan, Anna. *One True Thing*

- ℰ   Tan, Amy. *The Hundred Secret Senses*

ℰ *Deborah's Favorites*

"While outstanding writing skill was a major factor in my selection, the complete world created by the author was also very important. Whether it's one of fantasy or the unique way narrators see their world, I love to be carried away to a new place. Some of the books were chosen for the philosophical impact they had on me during a formative time of my life, like Castaneda and Lessing, which I read in college. For writing ability, Atwood, Erdrich, Kingsolver, and Marquez are my favorites."

- ℰ   Austen, Jane. *Pride and Prejudice*

- ℰ   Bradley, Marion Zimmer. *The Mists of Avalon*

- Castaneda, Carlos. *The Teachings of Don Juan*
- Hegi, Ursula. *Stones from the River*
- Lessing, Doris. *The Golden Notebook*
- Marquez, Gabriel Garcia. *Love in the Time of Cholera*
- Marquez, Gabriel Garcia. *One Hundred Years of Solitude*
- Proulx, E. Annie. *The Shipping News*
- Rutherfurd, Edward. *Sarum*
- Tolkien, J.R.R. *The Lord of the Rings*

ᶜᵉ Karen's Favorites

"I wasn't a big reader when I was young. That changed when I was fifteen and my mother introduced me to Agatha Christie—thus began my love affair with story. I've devoured books ever since. I read any work by Agatha Christie, Flannery O'Connor, and SARK."

- L'Engle, Madeleine. *A Wrinkle in Time*
- Lee, Harper. *To Kill a Mockingbird*
- Ludlum, Robert. *The Bourne Identity*
- O'Brien, Edna. *House of Splendid Isolation*
- Paretsky, Sara. *Guardian Angel*
- Quindlan, Anna. *Black and Blue*
- Uris, Leon. *Trinity*

ᶜᵉ Laurel's Favorites

"The first book that I remember having an impression on me was *A Wrinkle in Time* by Madeleine L'Engle. My mother sent it to me while I was at summer camp, and I read it by flashlight under the covers late into the night. I love being spellbound by a story and admire any author who is able to turn real life into art."

- Agee, James. *A Death in the Family*

- Atwood, Margaret. *Cat's Eye*

- Cather, Willa. *My Antonia*

- Cather, Willa. *O! Pioneers*

- Dickens, Charles. *Great Expectations*

- Guest, Judith. *Ordinary People*

- Harrison, Jim. *Farmer*

- King, Stephen. *Bag of Bones*

- McCourt, Frank. *Angela's Ashes*

- Smiley, Jane. *The Age of Grief*

- Tan, Amy. *The Joy Luck Club*

- Walker, Alice. *Temple of My Familiar*

Martha's Favorites

"My criteria for this list was to pick books that I had read more than once and that I had recommended to others. These are the authors I admire. These are the books that I loan only to the closest family members, the best of friends—people I am sure will return them."

- Atwood, Margaret. *The Robber Bride*

- Berg, Elizabeth. *What We Keep*

- Bradbury, Ray. *Fahrenheit 451*

- Hegi, Ursula. *Stones from the River*

- Irving, John. *A Prayer for Owen Meany*

- King, Stephen. *The Stand*

- Lee, Harper. *To Kill A Mockingbird*

- Pasternak, Boris. *Dr. Zhivago*

- Tan, Amy. *The Kitchen God's Wife*

- Tolkien, J.R.R. *The Lord of the Rings*

- Tyler, Anne. *Back When We Were Grownups*

- Tyler, Anne. *Saint Maybe*

✑ Sue's Favorites

"My reading selections have always paralleled my life. As a young girl I read classics by Louisa May Alcott and Laura Ingalls Wilder, then expanded my teenage world by reading books by Leon Uris and James Michener. Poetry balanced the textbooks I was assigned to read in college. As a young wife and mother I gleaned advice from Catherine Marshall, Haim Ginott, David Elkind, Chuck Swindoll, and James Dobson. And when my children grew up, my reading world became an open vista. I keep a database to record notes about each book I finish."

- Berg, Elizabeth. *What We Keep*

- Fitch, Janet. *White Oleander*

- Irving, John. *A Prayer for Owen Meany*

- Kingsolver, Barbara. *The Bean Trees*

- Kingsolver, Barbara. *The Poisonwood Bible*

- Lamb, Wally. *She's Come Undone*

- Lindbergh, Anne Morrow. *A Gift From the Sea*

- Morris, Mary McGarry. *Songs in Ordinary Time*

- Peretti, Frank E. *This Present Darkness*

- Peretti, Frank E. *Prophet*

- Shreve, Anita. *The Pilot's Wife*

- Uris, Leon. *Exodus*

- *The Bible*

Websites of Interest

SITE TITLE	ADDRESS	DESCRIPTION
Agent Research	www.agentresearch.com	*A resource to check or find an agent*
Association of Author's Representatives	www.aar-online.org	*Includes FAQ's, a Canon of Ethics, a newsletter, and related links*
Collected Stories	www.collectedstories.com	*Short stories on line*
FictionWriter's Connection	www.fictionwriters.com	*A variety of resources for fiction writers*
Freelance Writing	www.freelancewriting.com	*Resources, tools, guidelines, contests, and discussion forums for writers*
Literary Agents on the Web	www.literaryagents.org	*Articles about how to find an agent and information about agents who are seeking clients*
National Writer's Union	www.nwu.org	*A national resource for professional writers*
New Hampshire Writer's Project	www.nhwritersproject.org	*A nonprofit organization dedicated to fostering the literary community in the Granite State*
Poets and Writers	www.pw.org	*Includes articles and a classified section*
Publisher's Weekly	www.publishersweekly.com	*Offers information about publishing*
Romance Writers of America	www.rwanational.org	*Genre resources, author links, and contests*
Writer's Digest	www.writersdigest.com	*Articles, market information, contests, and submission guidelines*
The Writers Home	www.writershome.com	*A variety of resources for writers; includes information about freelancing*
Science Fiction and Fantasy Writers of America, Inc.	www.sfwa.org	*Craft and market resources for writers of science fiction and fantasy*
The Writer's Center	www.writer.org	*Information and resources related to writing*
Writers Write	www.writerswrite.com	*Lists writing, editing, and publishing related jobs*

About the Authors

Our individual journeys toward writing were diverse. Regardless of our childhood interests and the age at which we penned our first stories, writing is now the thread that binds us together.

✎ Karen Desrosiers

Karen didn't realize she was a writer until adulthood. Driven by creativity, with an imaginary life formed at a young age, she made up characters, stories, and worlds. Years of art lessons gave dimension to these worlds, but it wasn't until her first writing workshop that she knew she was a writer. Karen earned a B.S. in Computer Science and was a software engineer for more than fifteen years. During this time she wrote many technical and training manuals. She has been self-employed since 1992, dividing her time between software consulting and writing. However, after spending too many years in the high-tech world, Karen was suddenly hell-bent on leaving it for the writer's life. She writes a single-parenting column for *Our*

Times, a monthly woman's magazine, writes articles for the *Portsmouth Herald* and *Hampton Union*, and authored *Daytrips Québec* for Hastings House Books. Karen lives on the seacoast of New Hampshire with her young son. She can also sing the Oscar Mayer Bologna song in Spanish!

✎ Laurel Lloyd Earnshaw

Laurel grew up in a family of actors. At the age of five she debuted as Toto in *The Wizard of Oz*, and she continued to act through her teen years. Although thankful for the experience, she opted for a career that wouldn't require her to bark. Her desire to write solidified while a student at the University of Vermont, where several gifted professors inspired her to write. She earned a B.A. in English there in 1980 and an M.A. in Linguistics

and Writing at Northeastern University in 1987. Her first professional job as a writer was as a photojournalist, followed by a ten year stint as a corpo-

rate writer. Today she works as a freelance writer, and her essays have appeared on New Hampshire Public Radio and in such publications as the *Portsmouth Herald* and *The Aurora*, a newsletter she created with a friend and published for five years. Laurel enjoys photography, gardening, and outdoor sports. She lives in New Hampshire with her husband.

✐ *Charlene Pollano*

Charlene wrote her first illustrated novel when she was twelve. It was full of characters resembling Barbie and Ken, with GI Joe appearing intermittently. She received little creative encouragement along the way from nuns obsessed with sentence structure, high school English teachers with red pens, and college professors who preferred essays. She didn't return to her love of writing until twenty-five years later when an advertisement for a women's writing workshop called to her. The supportive feedback of the

instructor and other like-minded women helped Charlene's writing flourish and led to the creation of the Southern New Hampshire Women's Writing Group, of which she is a founding member. Charlene has been a high school counselor and parent educator for eighteen years. She has a B.S. in French Literature and an M.Ed. in Counseling. She has presented at conferences throughout New England on various topics related to adolescence and parenting. Charlene has published short stories and essays in various regional journals and is marketing her novel, *Dream Street*, which recently placed second runner-up in the Three Oaks Prize for Fiction. The parent of three young adults, she lives in New Hampshire with her husband.

❦ *Deborah Regan*

Deborah has dreamed of being a writer since third grade, and still has some poems and short stories written in elementary school. She wrote and read extensively all through college, then gave up writing for fifteen years, partly due to the writing philosophies of some college professors and partly to focus on a new career in counseling. She has a B.A. in English and an M.Ed. in Counseling. She has worked in higher education and industry as a career counselor and trainer for fifteen years. She returned to writing in her thirties and has participated in many writing workshops. She particularly enjoys writing short stories with quirky characters. Deborah is currently writing a novel set in the Netherlands, and

has published an essay in a national parenting magazine about adopting her daughter from Korea. Living in multiple states and countries has provided her with unique opportunities like learning Dutch and being a member of a girl's roping team. She lives on the seacoast of New Hampshire with her husband and young daughter.

❦ *Susan Wereska*

Sue's first fictional character, an imaginary friend named Puck, kept her company during her preschool years. Little did she know that in high school Shakespeare would introduce her to another character with the same name. Her first writing assignment, as fifth grade neighborhood news reporter for a student publication, launched her on a writing career that has focused mainly on education and children. Sue has enjoyed a variety of teaching experiences, from preschool through college, for more than twenty years, and she currently teaches language arts at the middle school level. She has an M.Ed. in Education and has presented workshops as an educational consultant throughout New England. Her writing

has been published in *The Journal* by the New England League of Middle Schools, where she is also the editor of *MidLines* and *HomeLines*, newsletters for educators and parents. Sue is a founding member of the Southern New Hampshire Women's Writing Group and is marketing her young adult novel, *No Goodbyes*. She loves to travel but always enjoys coming home to the Granite State where she skis, hikes, and bikes with her husband and adult children.

Bibliography

Angelou, Maya. *The Heart of a Woman*. New York: Random House, Inc., 1981.

Aronie, Nancy Slonim. *Writing from the Heart: Tapping the Power of Your Inner Voice*. New York: Hyperion, 1998.

Beasley, Angela. *Minutes from the Great Women's Coffee Club*. Tennessee: Walnut Grove Press, 1997.

Beren, Peter, and Brad Bunnin. *The Writer's Legal Companion*. Massachusetts: Perseus Books, 1998.

Berg, Elizabeth. *Escaping into the Open: The Art of Writing True*. New York: Perennial, 1999.

Brown, Renni, and David King. *Self-Editing for Fiction Writers*. New York: HarperCollins Publishers, 1993.

Burroway, Janet. *Writing Fiction: A Guide to Narrative Craft*. New York: HarperCollins, 1992.

Cameron, Julia. *The Vein of Gold: A Journey to Your Creative Heart*. New York: G. P. Putnam's Sons, 1996.

Cameron, Julia with Mark Bryan. *The Artist's Way: A Spiritual Path to Higher Creativity*. New York: G.P. Putnam's Sons, 1992.

Canfield, Jack, Mark Victor Hansen, and Bud Gardner, editors. *Chicken Soup for the Writer's Soul*. Florida: Health Communications, Inc., 2000.

Crawford, Brad, and the WD Staff. "Writer's Digest's 101 Best Web Sites For Writers." *Writer's Digest* (May 2000): 24-29.

DeSalvo, Louise. *Writing As A Way of Healing: How Telling Our Stories Transforms Our Lives*. Boston: Beacon Press, 1992.

Dillard, Annie. *The Writing Life*. New York: Harper and Row, 1989.

Goldberg, Bonni. *Room to Write*. New York: Penguin Putnam, 1996.

Horton, Tara A. "Queries That Made It Happen." *Guide to Literary Agents*. Cincinnati: Writer's Digest Books, 1998.

Jacobs, Ben and Helena Hjalmarsson, editors. *The Quotable Book*. New York: Lyons Press, 1999.

King, Stephen. *On Writing: A Memoir of the Craft*. New York: Scribner, 2000.

Krementz, Jill. *The Writer's Desk Calendar*. Germany, 2001.

Lamott, Anne. *Bird by Bird: Some Instructions on Writing and Life*. New York: Pantheon, 1994.

Lefcowitz, Dr. Allan, "A Guide to Managing Small Manuscript Critique Groups." Bethesda, Maryland: The Writer's Center, 1998.

Lerner, Betsy. *The Forest for the Trees*. New York: Penguin Putman Inc., 2000.

Moore, Lorrie. "Better and Sicker." *The Best Writing on Writing*. Edited by Jack Heffron. Ohio: Story Press, 1994.

Nickell, Kelly. "WD Interview-Beating the Odds with John Updike." *Writer's Digest*, Volume 82, #1. (January 2002): 34-35.

Pierce, Todd James. "The Practical Writer-Agents and the Internet." *Poets & Writers Magazine*. (May-June 2001): 70-73.

Ray, Robert J. *The Weekend Novelist*. New York: Dell, 1994.

Shindler, Dorman T. "In High Gear." *The Writer*, Volume 115, #1. (January 2002): 28-31.

Struckel Brogan, Katie. "The WD Interview—Surrendering with Laura Doyle." *Writer's Digest* (December 2001): 26-27.

Sumrall, Amber Coverdale. *Write to the Heart: Wit and Wisdom of Women Writers*. California: Crossing Press, 1992.

Ueland, Brenda. *If You Want to Write: A Book about Art, Independence, and Spirit*. 2nd ed. Saint Paul: Graywolf Press, 1987.

Woolf, Virginia. *A Room of One's Own*. New York: Harcourt Brace Jovanovich Inc., 1929.

Writer's Digest Books. *Writer's Market*. Cincinnati: Writer's Digest Books, 2000.

Index